IMAGES
of America

UNION PARISH

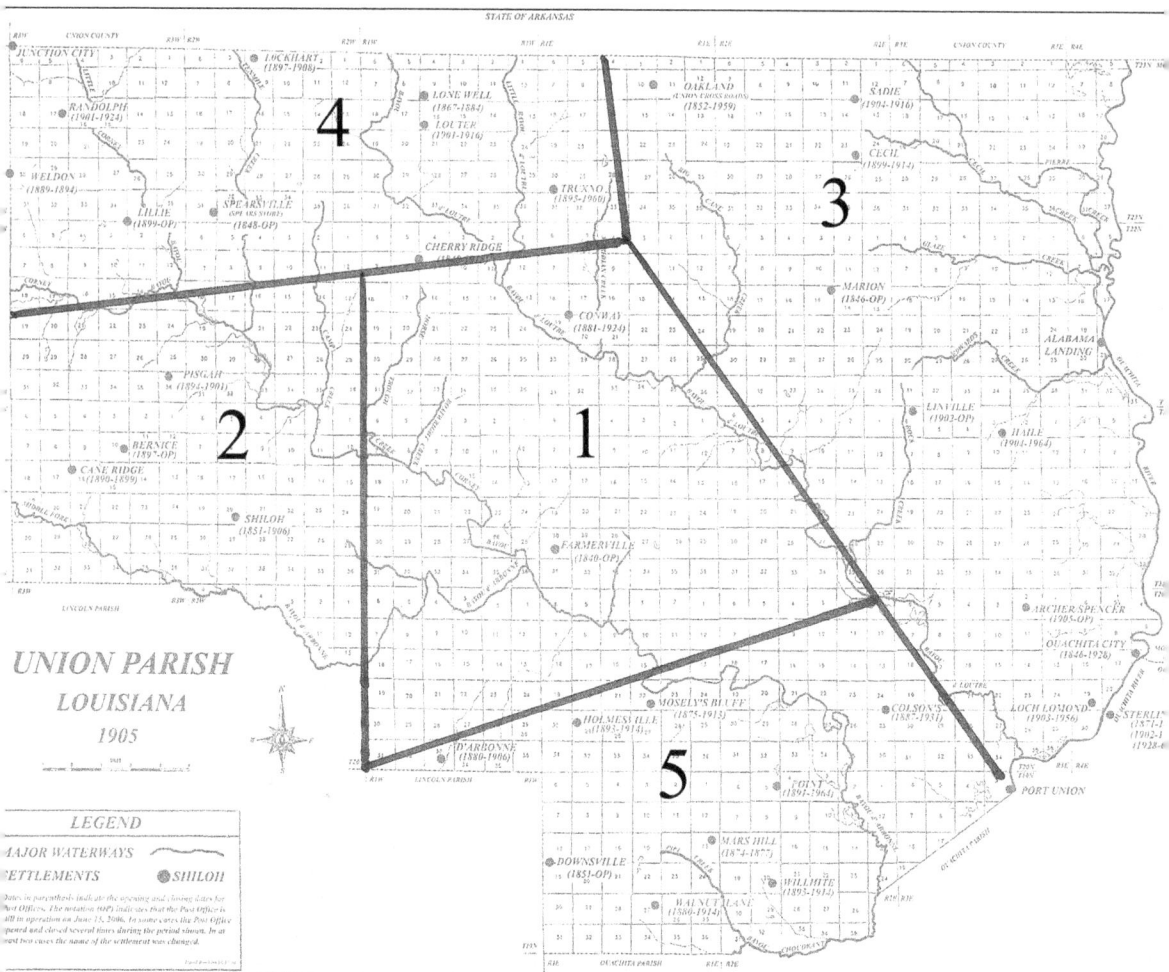

This map of Union Parish should give the reader an idea of the areas covered by each chapter of this history and the general layout of the parish. Chapter One is concerned with area No. 1, which is the central portion of the parish around its seat of Farmerville. Chapter Two deals with the southwestern portion of the parish, of which Bernice is the largest town and is labeled No. 2 on the map. Marion is the largest town in the eastern portion of the parish, labeled No. 3, and represented in Chapter Three. The area denoted by No. 4 is the northwestern part of the parish, of which Spearsville is the largest town; this is covered by Chapter Four. Chapter Five is concerned with the southern portion of the parish, of which Downsville is the largest town. It is labeled No. 5. (Courtesy Dave Dawkins.)

ON THE COVER: In the fall of each year, Farmerville High School celebrates a school homecoming. Graduates return annually to visit with teachers and old classmates. The homecoming parade is part of the celebration. The Farmerville High School majorettes and band lead the parade down Main Street in this 1965 photograph. The lead majorette is Mary Ann Eldridge. The next three are Jimmie Carolyn Wiley, Mary Jon Hallman and Jane Downs. (Courtesy Marilyn Ludwig.)

IMAGES
of America

UNION PARISH

W. Gene Barron

ARCADIA
PUBLISHING

Published by Arcadia Publishing
Charleston, South Carolina

Library of Congress Control Number: 2011942199

For all general information, please contact Arcadia Publishing:
Telephone 843-853-2070
Fax 843-853-0044
E-mail sales@arcadiapublishing.com
For customer service and orders:
Toll-Free 1-888-313-2665

Visit us on the Internet at www.arcadiapublishing.com

*To all who have gone on and left us with such a rich heritage and
to the ones who will follow to remind them of that heritage.*

CONTENTS

ACKNOWLEDGMENTS

When I first agreed to undertake the task of putting together a pictorial history of my home parish, I did not grasp the enormity of such an undertaking. There does not seem to be a concentration of Union Parish photographs in a depository anywhere. Therefore, I had to rely on individuals throughout the parish for photographs. Luckily, there were many who thought this was a worthy undertaking and contributed the time and effort to locate and share them—so many in fact that I am reluctant to try to name them for fear of leaving out someone. I would, however, like to thank Stephanie Antley Herrmann (director of the Union Parish Library), Jean Jones, Marilyn Ludwig, Cortez Laurence, and Tim Hudson for their assistance throughout this project.

My heartfelt word of thanks goes to Simone Monet-Williams and Jim Kempert at Arcadia who went well above their call of duty in assisting me in making this history possible.

INTRODUCTION

The earliest recorded white settlers of what would become Union Parish were members of the family of John Honeycutt who obtained land along Bayou D'Arbonne by a Spanish grant in the 1790s in a region known as Piney Hills. They were the only known white residents in the area until after 1800. John and Dorcas Stowe, Mills Farmer, Daniel Colvin, and William Lyles soon arrived. In 1814, George Feazel moved into the "Big Woods" area, and John Honeycutt Jr. immediately married Mary Feazel, George's daughter. In early 1837, Col. Matthew Wood arrived in Union Parish with a group of immigrants that included James Hayden Seale, David Ward, William Ham, Daniel Payne, and John Taylor. In 1837, Francis Turpin purchased land near Spearsville, but it is doubtful that he settled on the land. Others near Turpin's land were David G. Humphreys and Duncan McDougall.

By the late 1830s, settlers in the area petitioned the state for the creation of a parish of their own. Thanks to the efforts of Peter Harvey, Matthew Wood, Phillip Feazel, Daniel Payne, William Wood Farmer, Wiley Underwood, Stephen Colvin, and John Taylor, the state legislature created Union Parish on March 13, 1839, from the northwestern portion of Ouachita Parish. John Taylor was appointed by the legislature as the first parish judge, a position he held for the next decade.

Judge Taylor ordered the first meeting of the police jury on May 15, 1839, at the home of William Wilkerson at the mouth of Bayou Corney. Jury members elected at that meeting were John Newton Farmer (Ward 1), Jeptha Colvin (Ward 2), Phillip Feazel (Ward 3), Matthew Wood (Ward 4), Needham M. Bryan (Ward 5), Bridges Howard (Ward 6), and Don Pedro Aquilla Cook (Ward 7).

Col. Matthew Wood, newly elected president of the Union Parish Police Jury, purchased 160 acres of government land at $1.25 per acre for the purpose of establishing a parish seat that was to be named *Farmerville* after early resident and War of 1812 veteran Mills Farmer. The public square was chosen and marked off, as were adjacent town lots. The adjacent lots went on sale in July 1839.

During the next 20 years, the influx of settlers coming to Union Parish was tremendous, especially from Alabama, but also from Georgia, Mississippi, and some from Tennessee. Following trails established by Native Americans years earlier, immigrants flocked toward Union Parish. Reaching navigable streams, they then boarded steamboats to complete their journey. The main point of entry was a landing on the Ouachita River on the eastern boundary of Union Parish that was to become known as the Alabama landing. Some followed the Chickasaw trail from Montgomery through Tuscaloosa County on to Granada County, Mississippi, entering Desha County, Arkansas, and on south to Union Parish.

By 1850, numerous roads, ferries, and bridges had been established by the police jury. The towns of Ouachita City, Marion, Downsville, Spearsville, Shiloh, Cherry Ridge, D'Arbonne, and Spring Hill were formed, each having their own post offices. Farmerville had the most significant growth with doctors, lawyers, and a newspaper. Diverse shops and trades to fill the needs of the town folk were established.

There have been four native sons of Union Parish who have served as governors. William Wright Heard served from 1900 until 1904 and Ruffin Golson Pleasant from 1916 until 1920 (both from Shiloh), both as governors of Louisiana. George Washington Donaghey (born near Marion) served from 1909 until 1913, and Thomas Jefferson Terral served from 1925 until 1927, both as governors of Arkansas. W.W. Farmer served as lieutenant governor in the 1850s and died while holding that office on October 29, 1854.

Rural Union Parish has historically been an agriculturally oriented section of Louisiana with its residents deeply rooted in family and church traditions. Many have migrated away from the parish since the 1960s in search of better opportunities, but they are deeply rooted in ties to their Union Parish heritage and are well equipped to face the storms of life.

One

FARMERVILLE AND
CENTRAL UNION PARISH

Commissioners Matthew Wood, Philip Feazel, and Thomas Van Hook met to make a partial payment to contractor Robert Cook. In June 1840, the police jury allocated $2,980 for the construction of a courthouse and jail ($2,200 for the courthouse and $780 for the jail). The courthouse was described as being a brick structure 28 feet by 38 feet; it had two stories with a third story in the attic under a cypress-shingled hip roof. There were four doors in the building (one on each side), 13 windows with shutters, and a steeple that was added to the top. A second courthouse was built in about 1870. (Drawing by Carrie Armstrong.)

The third Union Parish courthouse, shown here, was built in 1904 and served the parish for nearly 55 years but met its demise in 1959 when "the powers that be" decided it was time for a more modern-looking structure. What a shame to lose such a beautiful, historically significant structure. (Courtesy Jeffy and Vicki Cole.)

Shown in this early photograph of Farmerville officials are, from left to right, Deputy Marshal Ed A. Phelps, Deputy Marshal Thad C. Griffin, Town Marshal Jesse Gillum, Night Marshal Walt Dykes, and Mayor Will E. Odom. (Courtesy Jeffy and Vicki Cole.)

The clerk of court's office during the 1920s was staffed by clerk of court James Monroe Dawkins, deputy clerk Sallie Preaus, and deputy clerk Aline Stancil. This sure looks like a modest office complex compared to that in existence today. (Courtesy clerk of court Doddie Eubanks.)

Fenner W. "Pat" Murphy served as Union Parish sheriff from 1924 until his death on March 4, 1939 at the age of 52. The conspiracy of 1933 seems to top the list of challenging cases that he had to contend with on his watch as sheriff. To complicate matters, Sheriff Murphy was at odds with Gov. Huey Long; therefore, funds were not available to hire needed deputies. George Miller Edwards and R.B. Mabry served as outside deputies while Deputy Jack Terral handled office duties. After his death his widow, the former Kathleen Turnage, finished out his term as sheriff with the help of George Miller Edwards and the other deputies. (Courtesy of Sheriff Bob Buckley.)

This photograph of some prominent residents of Farmerville was taken around the turn of the 20th century. They are, from left to right, (first row) N.B. Smith, Charles Roberts, Judge Robert B. Dawkins, and Fred F. Preaus; (second row) Harvey G. Fields, James M. Underwood, Edward W. Everett, Arthur Crow, John Sterling Crow, Tobin R. Hodge, Walter ?, and Clifton Mathews. (Courtesy Preaus Motor Company.)

This building first served as the jail and was built in the 1890s at a cost of $6,200 for the building and $885 for the installation of two jail cells. This is the oldest surviving public building in Union Parish. The second story of this building first served as a jail. Staves attached to the wall served as a stair case. Guards were stationed on the first floor. A latrine was later added under the staircase. When this photograph was taken, it housed the police jury. Today it serves as the Community Action Center. On June 19, 1884, Perry Melton and his son, William, were led from this jail and hanged in the Courthouse for the murder of John W. Cherry. (Courtesy of Stein Baughman.)

Heroice Long, who has the distinction of being the first woman to hold the office of police juror in Union Parish, had the honor of cutting the ribbon that formally opened the new courthouse in February 1962. Senator Russell Long spoke at the courthouse dedication to a crowd of hundreds. The Farmerville High School band provided the music for the affair. (Courtesy Linda Long Pardue.)

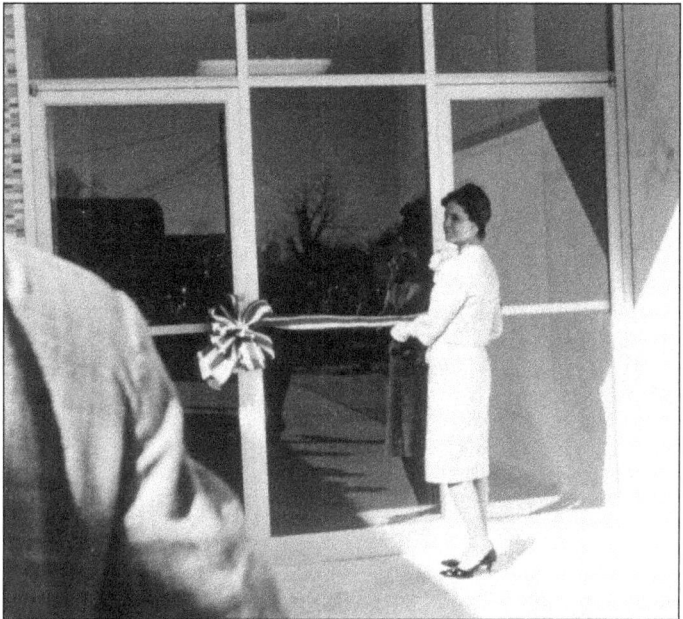

The members of the Union Parish Police Jury present at the new courthouse dedication on February 11, 1962, are, from left to right, (first row) Cona Spillers (Ward 8), Grover Davis (Ward 9), J. Elton Johnson (Ward 6), Eugene Pearson (Ward 4), and C. Otha Brown (Ward 2); (second row) Dennis Long (president), John Henry Caskey (Ward 1), E.R. Rogers (Ward 7), Glover Rockett (Ward 3), and James Brashier (secretary). Wince Farrar, police juror for Ward 10, is absent. (Courtesy Linda Long Pardue.)

Dennis Long won the sheriff's election in 1964. He and his deputies are being sworn in by Judge James Robert Dawkins (left). From left to right, they are Dennis Long, George Miller Edwards, Eugene Patterson, Meredith L. Ferguson, Glenn Barron, Caldwell Harris, J.T. Rockett, Bobby Tucker, and Alma Gray Taylor. The newly elected sheriff's father, John Emmett Long, is sitting on the bench in front witnessing the swearing in. (Courtesy Linda Long Pardue.)

Police jurors elected in 1971 are taking their oath given by Judge Dawkins. They are, from left to right, J.E. Johnson (Ward 6), Doris Kyle Russell (Ward 9), Almer Rockett (Ward 10), Kelton Howard (Ward 7), John Henry Caskey (Ward 1), Ruffin Beaird (Ward 3), Eugene Pearson (Ward 4), Walter Hinton (Ward 5), Brooks Jones (Ward 2), and Cona Spillers (Ward 8). (Courtesy Union Parish Police Jury.)

The Farmerville train depot served the Missouri Pacific system until the 1960s. The Rock Island also sent trains to Farmerville for a while before the rail system was abandoned. This photograph was taken on the occasion of a car-train wreck in about 1957. Alvin Green, who was in the car behind Mildred Hayes, said that she was forced to stop on the tracks because of traffic as the Rock Island train came to Farmerville and hit her car and knocked it into the ditch. Her car is seen at left. Grayson Odom's Magnolia Oil bulk plant also can be seen at left. (Courtesy Sheriff Bob Buckley.)

Dr. Jordan Gray Taylor brought the first automobile to Farmerville in 1911. It was an old EMF, which he purchased for $1,050. (EMF was a volume automobile maker in the early 1900s.) Many young men took turns riding in the car the day it arrived. The steering wheel is on the right-hand side. Those pictured are, from left to right, Walker Wallace, unidentified, Sam Wallace Jr., and Alonza "Keencutter" Booth. Dr. Taylor graduated from Louisville Medical College on March 10, 1894. (Courtesy Preaus Motor Company.)

This building was constructed in 1928 to house the Union Parish School Board. It was located on the block east of the courthouse. The Parish Public Library shared a room in this building when the library first started. In the years before its construction, the school board met in a small building located on the southeast corner of the town square. (Courtesy Marilyn Ludwig.)

By March 1956, public interest was such that parish-wide library service was established in a portion of the Union Parish School Board building. In December, a parish-wide three-mill tax was passed for the continuation of the service. On October 29, 1966, the tax was renewed, and .75 mill was dedicated for construction of a permanent home for the library to be located on the lot where the Smith Hotel once stood. The formal opening was held on April 20, 1969. The total cost of the building was $180,000 financed by local funds and matching funds from the state library through the Library Services and Construction Act. At present, the book/media collection numbers over 62,000. (Courtesy Union Parish Library.)

The Boy Scout hut was built by John D. Ludwig and served many generations of scouts who harbor fond memories of it and their scoutmaster Larce Holder. Troop 16 was sponsored by the Farmerville Lions Club for many years. Sadly, the building burned in the 1970s. (Courtesy Marilyn Ludwig.)

Members of the Farmerville Lion's Club during the 1960s include, from left to right, (first row) Roy Kennedy, Bobby G. Miller, Alvin Y. Green, W.A. Colvin, Robert R. James, Wilson Albritton Jr., "Skinnie" Malone, and A.B. Post Jr.; (second row) John Waguon, Rev. T.W. Waggoner, Fred Preaus, Dr. Billy Terral, William Ray Alexander, Jack Turnage, Ramond "Red" Albritton, Joe Brantley, L.C. Allen, and Willie H. Barron; (third row) unidentified, "Cotton" Allen, J.T. Spencer, John Caldwell, Jack Hill, Russell Adams, Ben Lee, James Wiley, C.C. Murphy, Red Murphy, Dr. ?, and Bryant James. (Courtesy Farmerville Lions Club.)

K.D. Kilpatrick is pictured in front of Kilpatrick's Funeral Home in about 1960, accompanied by a Union Parish sheriff's deputy. After the death of their father in 1954, K.D. and Tex took over the family business. An employee hired to take the death calls at night slept upstairs. (Courtesy Kilpatrick's Funeral Homes.)

Born with the Midas touch, everything Jefferson Davis Baughman touched seemed to turn to money. He successfully ran a large plantation and operated cotton warehouses on the local bayous. He established the Farmerville State Bank in Farmerville on June 15, 1903, and opened it in September of that year. The bank suspended operations in 1933. (Courtesy Stein Baughman.)

Mose Hartman owned this hotel from 1884 until Rodelle Tugwell bought it in 1921 and changed the name to the Tugwell Hotel. It was *the* place to go while visiting Farmerville. The food served there was acclaimed far and wide. Gov. Huey Long was a guest there in 1931. As a young girl, Marilyn Ramsey was awed by this man dressed in a white suit and sporting a walking cane on his arm, which he did not need. Legend has it that when Governor Pleasant was a small boy, he fell from the pecan tree in the backyard and broke his arm. Rodelle operated the hotel until his wife died on November 6, 1961, when he passed the property to their three children. (Courtesy Marilyn Ludwig.)

Fred Preaus bought the Mitchell Ford dealership on the north side of Farmerville in 1933. In 1946, Preaus erected a new building for his motor company at its present location, and his brother Harry joined the company. They enjoyed many years of successful business until their retirements. Today, Joe and John Preaus have the honor of owning and operating the oldest business in the town of Farmerville. The Preaus Motor Company employees in 1946 are, from left to right, Troy Ham, J.D. Gillum, Fletcher Ramsey, Elgin Dean, Ishmal Derks, Lawrence D. Carroll, Harry Preaus, Fred Preaus, Willie Green, C.R. Tucker, Sammie Simons, Raymond Warren, Luther Warren, and unidentified. (Courtesy Preaus Motor Company.)

Dan Green and Draughn Smith owned and operated a livestock sale barn on the lot where they later built the CITGO Station, which Smith operated. At some point, Fred Preaus bought the station, and Elgin Dean and Fletcher Ramsey ran it for him. The station was later demolished to make room for a new parking lot for Preaus Motor Company. (Courtesy Preaus Motor Company.)

Jake Long bought the Pontiac dealership from Benny Patton in about 1958. He later acquired the Oldsmobile dealership, and built a larger facility to display his cars in 1967. Long Motor Company held its grand opening in the new building in July of that year. The employees pictured are, from left to right, Bo Craighead (mechanic), Fred White (salesman), Vernon McCorly (salesman), Heroice Long (secretary), Hazel Long (secretary), Jake Long (owner), Johnny Wilson (mechanic), Henry Clay Atkins (mechanic), unidentified (mechanic), and Duke Fields (worker). (Courtesy Linda Long Pardue.)

In the early 1930s, Herbert Green and his father, Murry H. Green, began running this service station when Emmett Lee Ward, who owned the station, elected to take over a Lion Oil station. The elder Green had taken over the Esso bulk plant. In 1948, Herbert Green was approached by Jack and James Hill, who owned the Gulf bulk plant in Farmerville, about building a new service station on the corner of Main Street and the Marion Highway and taking on Gulf products. Green accepted the offer, and after moving his family home from the property, he built a new station with three mechanics' bays across the street from the old one. Green operated this station until his retirement. (Courtesy Diane Green Smith.)

The Smith Hotel stood one block west of Main Street and was built by Dr. C.H. Jameson in 1905 as his family's residence. In 1916, Samuel B. Smith and Amelia (Kennedy) Smith bought the property and operated it as a hotel until it burned in 1943. The Union Parish Library is located on the lot today. (Courtesy Mattie Gray Bird.)

Located just east of Farmerville, this home was built in 1902 by Capt. Jefferson Davis Baughman. The man hired by Captain Baughman to construct the home was John Lorenzo "Preacher" Hicks, an ordinary carpenter who was as much at home driving nails as he was preaching. Many were amazed that he could have built such an immaculate and diverse home in just 13 months. The style is described as "Steamboat Gothic" or "Queen Anne" and seems appropriate for the home of a steamboat man. Upon completion, Captain Baughman filled the house with imports from Europe. In 1979, the home was abandoned and fell into disrepair. Pat and Kay Carroll eventually bought the home and are at present restoring it and converting it into a bed and breakfast. (Courtesy of Pat and Kay Carroll.)

The road was paved from Farmerville to Marion in the summer of 1931. The young men hired for the job are, from left to right, (kneeling and sitting) Steve Huckaby, J.L. "Bud" Jones, Henry Murphy, George Matthews, and Harry Preaus Jr.; (standing) unidentified, Joe B. Stewart, Charlie Stewart, Phillip Derks, and "Cornfield" Carter. (Courtesy Preaus Motor Company.)

There were two steamships named *Rosa B*. Farmerville residents Capt. Lazarus Brunner Jr. and John M. Rabun had the first one built in July 1879 in Cincinnati. It was a large steamer that could easily glide in 20 inches of water. It made a name for itself as one of the fastest on the Ouachita. On December 30, 1881, she burned above the mouth of D'Arbonne. The *Rosa B* shown above was a much smaller steamer and was built in 1895 by Cicero Bearden. After Bearden's premature death in 1896, Capt. Oscar Baughman acquired the boat and operated it until February 16, 1901, when the little steamer burned while docked at Farmerville landing. Passengers and crew sleeping on board managed to escape. (Courtesy of Stein Baughman.)

The *Mattie* was owned and operated by Marion Willis Wilson, who lived in Farmerville. The *Mattie* operated mainly between Monroe and Moseley Bluff and on Bartholomew Bayou, transporting freight, such as staves, and occasionally passengers. *Mattie* was a relatively small steamboat. Wilson continued to operate the steamboat until about 1911. In 1912, he was elected tax assessor of Union Parish, a position he held until his death in December 1919. Standing on top of the *Mattie* at right is Capt. Willis Wilson. The lady on the left of the forward deck is Maranda Calk Hicks. Her husband, Wesley, is the second person from the left. Fourth from the left is Robert Terral. Pete and Fannie Taylor Skains are standing on the shore at right. (Courtesy Charles Terral.)

On June 25, 1935, a group of men from Civilian Conservation Corps Company 1440 near Marion started a new camp three and one-fifth miles northeast of Farmerville that was later designated as Company 4409. In that year, Camp No. 4409 was dedicated to control soil erosion. Men and officers of Company 4409 posed for this photograph. Frank Yelton (shown in the third row and noted by a check mark) was one of the officials in charge of the camp. Others known to be in Camp No. 4409 were Ben Doster, Raymond Turnage, Eugene Robert, Otis Tugwell, John F. Ramsey, Layelle Doster, Jack Hammonds, Gray Robinson, W.E. Price, Joe B. Aulds, and Purvis Christian. Each morning, crews of the 4409 boarded trucks and were transported to locations throughout western Union Parish to work on assigned jobs. The men were proud of the opportunity to contribute, accomplished meaningful tasks, and were thankful for the badly needed income for their families. (Courtesy John Yelton.)

New Enterprise School was located southeast of Farmerville in the Enterprise community and was another of those schools first established after the public school system was initiated. Not to be confused with the old community of Enterprise at Rocky Branch, the school was designated New Enterprise. (Courtesy Union Parish Library.)

Crossroads was another of the first schools established after the public school system began. Nannie Heard started her teaching career at Crossroads. She recalled having to turn school out early each day to avoid disruption by some rowdy boys who came by the school after they got off from work. (Courtesy Union Parish Library.)

Another of the first public schools established in Union Parish was Salem, which was located a few miles northeast of Farmerville. When the school closed, the students transferred to Farmerville High School. (Courtesy Union Parish Library.)

Hopewell School was located some six or seven miles east of Farmerville at the intersection of Louisiana Highway 828 and Union Parish Road 7763 when the public school system began. The exact date it was started is unknown, but it was in existence in the early 1900s. In 1944, the students transferred to Farmerville High, and the school disbanded. (Courtesy Terry Lee Pratt.)

Pictured here are students attending Hopewell School in about 1925. The students are, from left to right, (first row) Kathleen Albritton, Woodrow Hudson, James Dean, Ethell Albritton, Metter Nolan, Boyd Albritton, Mildred Albritton and George Scarborough; (second row) Stells B. Scarborough, Annie Mae Taylor, Inez Albritton, Edna Hayes, Anna Nolan, Estell Albritton, Retha Cole, Mattie Lee Ward and Kalvin Dean; (third row)Evelyn Albritton, Velma Dean, Audry Cole, Drue Goyne, John Lee Albritton, John Hudson, Irven Albritton and Horace Neal; (forth row) Sarah Albritton, Evelyn Hudson, Katie Goyne, George Ham, Taylor Albritton, Brewer Cole, June Hudson, J.B. Albritton, Snake Hayes and Tommie Goyne; (fifth row) Cora Albritton, Lelia Hudson, Sally Goyne, Grover Sharp, Clifton Albritton, Duke Hayes, Wilburn Albritton, Henry Albritton and Herman Albritton. The teachers were Hull and Brasher. (Courtesy of Terry Lee Pratt.)

Education at Tugwell City in 1936 consisted of a two-room schoolhouse. The first, second, and third grades were taught in one room by Catherine Canteberry, and the fourth, fifth, sixth, and seventh grades (shown here) were taught by Maurene Breazeal. The teachers boarded at the Tugwell Hotel. Unfortunately, the students' names are not known. After consolidation with the public schools, the students at Tugwell City transferred to Farmerville High School. (Courtesy Maurene Breazeal Barron.)

Children attending Central School (located in the Cherry Ridge community) are pictured in about 1929. (This was Faye Brantley Futch's first teaching assignment.) Those pictured are, in order of number on photograph, Flora Nell Neal, George C. Phelps, Gloria Jean Williams, Treva Phelps, Merle Tucker, Faylene Norris, Christine Ferguson, Florence Jean Odom, Carol Nuvkirk, Mildred Thomas, Jessie Thomas, Madeline Waldrop (teacher), Nulan Odom, Arnold Thomas, Vivian Ferguson, Clarice Odom, Chloe Phelps, Lora Lee Turnage, Latance Phelps, Fay Brantley (teacher), Rudolph Tucker, Howard Tucker, Kenneth Tucker, Lona Grace Odom, Ruby Jean Turnage, Norvell Turnage, Kathleen Turnage, Ollie Vee Tucker, Norma Odom, Ivelle Odom, Effie Ree Norris, Harold Turnage, Vance Turnage, S.E. Williams, J.C. Williams, Victor Philps, Darrell Tucker, Victor Williams, Rivis Tucker, Jerald Futch, Robert Tucker, B.E. Neal, Perkle Tucker, Dean Murphy Davis, Laymond Odom, Egbert Odom, Wilbur Tucker, Jack Phillips, Raymond Odom, Frances Williams, and Carnis Williams. (Courtesy Faye Futch.)

Students in the 1948–1951 class at Union Parish Training School are shown here. Kneeling from left to right are Geneva Lee, Lola Bright, Della Williams, Verdell Williams, and Earline Fields. Unfortunately those standing are unidentified. (Courtesy Verdell Ventroy.)

This photograph of Farmerville High School (built in 1925) was taken before the gymnasium was added. The structure was demolished in 1963 to make way for the building that stands today. (Courtesy Jeffy and Vicki Cole.)

This Baptist Church building was constructed in 1853 and later remodeled with educational wings added to both sides. It had two front doors—one for the women and one for the men. The first pastor was Rev. Elias George. (Courtesy Marilyn Ludwig.)

One of the first acts of the police jury upon its organization was to donate an acre of land for a Methodist church. The church building was not constructed for nearly 50 years. The Methodists believed in "paying as you go," and it was not until they had the money necessary for the construction that it was built. The second building is pictured here. The third and present building was completed in 1960. (Courtesy Ron Downing.)

The congregation at the First Baptist Church posed for this photograph in 1941. Notice the absence of young men in the group. World War II demanded their service during the years between 1941 and 1945. (Courtesy of Marilyn Ludwig.)

The Woodlawn Baptist Church was established in 1880 and is located seven miles southwest of Farmerville. The deacons during Rev. W.W. Moore's pastorate are Will Jones, F.C. Williams, and Louis Fields. The choir president is Dorothy Gibson. The deaconess president is Essie Cottingham, and the home missions president is Eula Jenkins. (Courtesy Verdell Ventroy.)

The Gum Spring Baptist Association was organized in 1872. Early participants included (first row) Lucy Davis, Rev. Clyde Oliver, Rev. W.W. Rutland (moderator), and Harrison D.C. Douglas; (second row) unidentified, Blanche Sims, two unidentified, and Georgia Williams; (third row) ? Singleton, unidentified, Hazel Douglas, John Q. Watley, and unidentified; (fourth row) unidentified, J.K. Haynes, and ? Meadows; (fifth row, standing) Jessie Bilberry (principal), ? McDaniel (principal), and Algia Payne. (Courtesy Verdell Ventroy.)

This photograph was taken on July 4, 1888, by J.G. Davis, artist and photographer of Farmerville, at a picnic given by the Good Intent Lodge, Knights of Honor, at Scott's Bluff near Farmerville. During its heyday, Scotts Bluff was a regular stop for steamboats traveling from West Monroe bringing goods to the area and taking produce to market. (Author's collection.)

The Prince Hall Affiliation of the Masonic Lodge in the Woodlawn community was organized in the early 1950s. The members are (first row) Shellie Spivey, Will Jones (worshipful master), and Everett Lewis; (second row) F.C. Williams, ? Everett, Jack Griffin, Jacob Payne, Rev. George Allen Carr, Lovell Lewis, Roy Warren, and Prentiss Gibson. (Courtesy Verdell Ventroy.)

The Union Parish Training School Glee Club's music director in 1950–1951 was Annie Dean Payne. Those in the club were, from left to right, (first row) Willie Mae Roberts, Juanita Furlough, Verdell Williams, Annie Dean Payne, Jean Claiborne, and two unidentified; (second row) Francine Sawyer, ? Mason, Maurice Brunner, Addie Woods, and Martha Burch; (fourth row) Earnestine Mack, Fayola Sims, Reola Dawkins, Sherman Carter, Joe Dixson, Warren Hendricks, unidentified, Ira Johnson, Breard Williams, Lola Bright, John A. Taylor, Frankie Lee Bilberry, and Bobbie Moss. (Courtesy of Verdell Ventroy.)

At the beginning of World War II, the United States began rigorous training of troops throughout the country. The cavalry from Fort Riley, Kansas, held maneuvers in and around Farmerville in 1941. Complacent since World War I, which had utilized mules and horses to a large extent, the army began training with them again. It was not long before mechanization took over and the Army quickly retired the animals. The soldiers were welcome in the area and invited into homes for meals and to take bathes. At night, the soldiers retired to their encampment, which was set up a short distance from Farmerville. (Courtesy Marilyn Ludwig.)

The communication center for the maneuvers was set up on September 6–9, 1941, along the side of the *Gazette* office. This seems to be a meager center for such an operation, but the US armed forces would make tremendous advances over the next few years to meet the demand of what would become a world war. (Courtesy Marilyn Ludwig.)

The United States was not prepared to go to war when Congress declared it against Germany on December 11, 1941. Notable in this 1941 photograph of solders on maneuvers in Farmerville are the World War I uniforms and machine gun. The US Army had a lot of advancements to make before sending soldiers into battle. (Courtesy Marilyn Ludwig.)

After much political wrangling, the state legislature approved the construction of the south's largest manmade lake in Union Parish. In 1958, the D'Arbonne Lake Commission purchased the flowage rights for the Lake D'Arbonne project. A total of 14,667.26 acres of land had to be purchased before construction of the dam and spillway could be started. The clearing of the site of the structure began in May 1960, the project was completed in the fall of 1963, and the floodgates were closed in January 1964. The lake was stocked with crappie, channel catfish, bluegill, and bass. This view of Lake D'Arbonne was taken shortly after its construction. By the time of this writing, the trees shown in the upper portion of the lake are gone and only a few stumps remain. (Courtesy Union Parish Library.)

Two

BERNICE AND
SOUTHWESTERN UNION PARISH

Capt. C.C. Henderson, of the Arkansas Southern Railroad, bought land in the area of Union Parish called the Big Woods from Allen Lowery and Dave Cole on which he proposed to build a town. He established a sawmill and began producing lumber to construct the first buildings in the town. The company office is seen to the left with the cone-shaped roof. The sawmill managers were James C. Love and Jackson Westbrook. (Courtesy Bernice Depot Museum.)

Captain Henderson located his lumber mill and office building beside his railroad tracks just north of the town. The building surely served as a lumber office as well as a depot for his train. The office and staff are shown here. As soon as the mill was established, Henderson started cutting lumber from the virgin pine in the area for construction of the town he envisioned. The town was laid out, and he started selling lots. (Courtesy Bernice Historical Society.)

Captain Henderson boarded with the Allen B. Lowery family while laying out the town, and he named it Bernice after Lowery's daughter. Captain Henderson found ready buyers for his lots in Bernice. On April 18, 1899, the town of Bernice was incorporated and Jake Cruze named mayor. As a gift to the town, Captain Henderson reserved one lot, which is known today as Oakhurst Park. (Courtesy Bernice Depot Museum.)

This photograph was taken in the office of the Arkansas Southern Railroad Depot in Bernice in 1906. Those identified are Charles A. Carroll (standing in the back at right), Dr. George R. Carroll (seated in front), depot agent Ben Stratford (seated at his desk), and Jesse B. Hollis (standing in the back to the left). (Courtesy Ted Carroll.)

The Bernice depot is shown as it appeared after rail service was discontinued through Bernice and its future was at peril. The town of Bernice acquired the property, restored the building, and has turned it into the Bernice Depot Museum. (Courtesy Bernice Historical Society.)

The Bank of Bernice was founded in 1901. On the far right is Richard Tubb Moore. The first officers of the bank (not pictured) were James R. Fuller (president), his son Young S. Fuller (cashier), and W.F. Grafton (assistant cashier). Others who have served as president are Richard T. Moore, George W. James, Young S. Fuller, D.A. Pollock, Dr. C.C. Colvin, L.H. Pratt, Dr. M. Wick Laurence Sr., W. Van Salley, and Henry F. Walden. (Courtesy Wanda Fuller.)

This photograph of the interior of the first Bank of Bernice building was taken in the 1920s. In the teller windows are Lawton Pratt (left) and Shapley Fitzgerald (right). President of the bank Y.S. Fuller stands in front. (Courtesy Bernice Depot Museum.)

Maggie Adcock, daughter of Bernice photographer J.B. Adcock, became Bernice's first telephone operator when the service was established by J.W. Pickens in the town shortly before 1920. (In 1921, Maggie married Garland Austin.) A few years later, Bell Telephone Company bought the telephone system. (Courtesy Bernice Depot Museum.)

By the early 1900s, shoppers and visitors alike swarmed to the newly formed town of Bernice and hitched their wagons and horses in this lot while in town. It is difficult to imagine the mess that had to be contended with. (Courtesy Bernice Historical Society.)

By the early 1900s, Bernice had become a thriving town, as demonstrated by this photograph of the Bernice Hardware and Furniture Store. Notable is the assortment of farm tools for sale in front and to the left side of the store. (Courtesy Bernice Historical Society.)

Bobby Lee St. John established the first Ford dealership in Bernice around 1920. He lacked the showroom that is featured at automobile dealerships today, but he seems to have done well in the new venture. Automobiles were fast replacing the horse and wagon by the 1920s—and gas was cheap. (Courtesy Bernice Historical Society.)

The Bank of Bernice, the E.C. Colvin clothing store, and M.A. Talbot were located on Main Street in Bernice and were well established when this photograph was taken in about 1910. The Bank of Bernice was established in 1909 immediately after Captain Henderson started selling lots in the town. (Courtesy Bernice Historical Society.)

Willie C. Tanner operated this Esso service station in Bernice during the 1930s for Dr. Jessie Tanner, who owned the station. By the 1930s, service stations such as this one were in demand all over, as more and more families began to rely on the automobile instead of the horse and buggy. Malvin Liggin is pictured in the foreground. (Courtesy Bernice Historical Society.)

This is the original building occupied by Kilpatrick's Funeral Home in Bernice. Effie Kilpatrick became the first woman mortician licensed in the state of Louisiana and drove to Bernice from Farmerville every day to operate the home in Bernice. Her husband, Edgar Noel Kilpatrick, ran the home in Farmerville. (Courtesy Bernice Historical Society.)

The employees of Salley Grocery Company in 1942 are Lyle Gresham, C.T. Salley, Jack Salley, Van Salley, Fred Salley, Carroll Farrar, L.P. Whiteside, Cobin Platt, M.A. Johnson, Perry Tubbs, James Salley, W.L. Lee, T.E. Newton, Faye Burns, George Grafton, J.B. Farrar, Harry Shackleford, Virginia Lee Faulkner, Dan Watson, Earnestine Hollis, Evelyn Lee, Gladys Moncrief, Sted Weir, James Buckley, "Bo" Stokes, unidentified, Bennett Farrar, Dendy Elliott, "Pete" Teterson, Borden Rockett, four unidentified, "Soda Pop" Lindsey, Doyle Ferguson, three unidentified, C.A. Harris, John Frank Jone, three unidentified, and Charles Hildridge. The remainder of the employees are unidentified. (Courtesy Jackie Dickerson.)

In 1938, J.Y. Green came to Bernice and bought the Welch Motor Company from George Welch, who had a sub-dealership selling Chevrolets from Fuller Chevrolet of Dubach. A year or so later he acquired a full dealership. In 1954 Green wanted to sell the company but decided to offer it to his son, Alvin, first. At the time Alvin had the Pontiac dealership in Farmerville, but decided to sell it and move to Bernice and take over the Chevrolet dealership. In 1964, J.Y. and Alvin demolished the old building and built the modern building pictured here. Alvin sold the dealership to Russell Adams in about 1986. Russell closed the doors a few years later when General Motors was cutting small dealerships. (Courtesy Alvin Green.)

In the summer of 1943, F.C. Platt bought the Jitney Jungle from his father-in-law, W.L. Key. In 1944, he sold the store and opened Platt's store, which was a dry goods and grocery store less a meat market. He enjoyed a successful business for nearly 40 years, closing the establishment in May 1982. (Courtesy Kathryn Ward.)

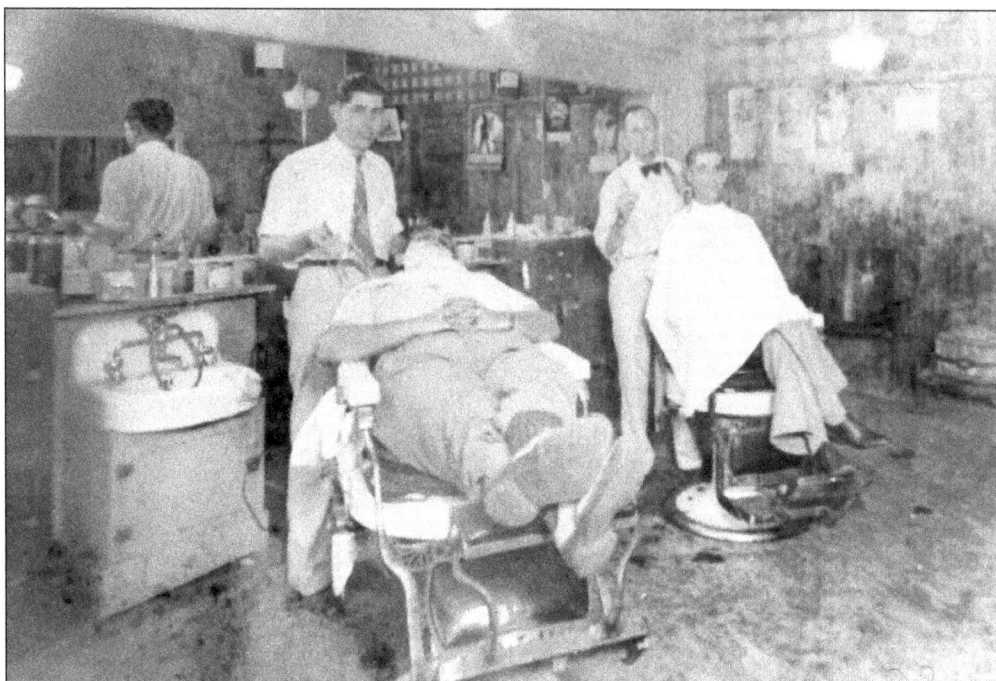

The barbershop in Bernice in 1941 was operated by Clifton McIntosh (left) and Frank Gray (right). Clifton related that when he began barbering in the late 1930s, haircuts were 35¢. During weekdays, he had very little business because most of his customers were farmers who only came to town on Saturday. He started cutting hair before daylight on Saturdays and did not finish until after 9:00 p.m. There were still saloons in Bernice at the time, and most of the men getting haircuts after dark were drunk. Many a week, Clifton said that he made more than the president of the bank. Barbershops are becoming a rarity in modern times. Billy McIntosh continues his uncle's business today, but his breed seems to be on the verge of becoming extinct. (Courtesy Billy McIntosh.)

In 1958, Louis Perry Whiteside opened his appliance store in Bernice on the north side of Main Street in a rented building. A few years later, he built his own store a block north of Main Street. He enjoyed a very successful business until his death in 1984, at which time the family disposed of the property. (Courtesy Mary Ackel Odom.)

Donald Lindsey owned and operated the warehouses at top right in Bernice that were used to store government surplus grain and other commodities during the 1950s–1970s. He also owned cotton gins in Bernice and Spearsville during the 1940s–1950s. The Bernice cemetery is at lower right. (Courtesy Donna McDowell.)

Bernice was a bustling town during the 1950s. Located on the intersection of the railroad and Louisiana State Highways 167 and 2, it seemed to offer more new business opportunities than even the parish seat of Farmerville. At one time, it supported three automobile dealerships and two sawmills. (Courtesy Bernice Depot Museum.)

Shown in this photograph are the following members of the Bernice High School graduation class of 1912, from left to right: (first row) Emma Thaxton, Seabron Lee Digby, Maggie Lowery, Etta Hollis, John Tom Hollis, Nan Moore, and Lafe Ferguson; (second row) principal G.W. Newton, Ellis L. Cook, Edward F. Hollis, Izora Wainwright, Fair Butler, Tom Foster Digby, Kirtley Touchstone, William Grafton, and Tommie Miller. (Courtesy Bernice Historical Society.)

The Bernice football team of 1923–1924 includes, from left to right, (front row) Alton Thompson, Allen Buckley, Clifton Flurry, Lowery Lowery, Sidney Pratt, Homer Thompson, and Travis Hollis; (second row) Presley Barrett, Fuller Smith, Martin Porter, Howard Graves, Morelle Hollis, Erskine Gaston, and Carl Shaddock. Coach Long, who coached the team, is not pictured. (Courtesy Bernice Depot Museum.)

The Bernice High School band of 1929 includes, from left to right, (first row) Clyde C. Colvin and Van H. Burns; (second row) Leanard Goss, Donald Lindsey, Van Pratt, Stanford Breazeal, Leonard Green, Seth Shackleford, Joe Bolen, and unidentified; (third row) band director Guy McDonald, Wick Laurence, Clyde Barrett, Everett Clary, Gid Grafton, Max Miller, Houston Bailey, and Wallace Kindle. (Courtesy Bernice Historical Society.)

This 1931 Bernice High baseball team won the North Louisiana rally by defeating Ouachita High but was defeated by Jefferson High in the state finals. The teams did not compete according to the size of the school in those days. The players are, from left to right, (first row) Troy Shackleford, Lyle Gresham, M.C. Still, Dale Goss, Chic Burns, Max Akins, and Donald Lindsey (manager); (second row) Carl Akins, Everett Albritton, Barham Sterling, John Porter, Grady Farrar, Curtis Green, and Coach H.S. Wasson. (Courtesy Bernice Historical Society.)

The 1954 Bernice High School baseball team sported a record of 22 wins and only 6 losses. Shown from left to right are (first row) Bobby Till (catcher), Gerald Glover (right field), Joe Green (first base), Ted Farrar (pitcher), Larry Elliott (left field), Lynn Skinner (right field), Kenneth Lee (first base), and Paul Salley (second base); (second row) Thomas "Lefty" Smith (assistant coach), Ben Carroll (head coach), Billy Bryom (second base), Jimmy Bowen (catcher), Charles Glen Byrom (infield), Billy Gene Pearson (second base), Wayne Tubbs (third base), Gene Gray (center field), Van Kelly (pitcher), Graydon Fitzgerald (pitcher), Bobby Copeland (pitcher), and John Tom Grafton (manager). (Courtesy Bernice Historical Society.)

The 1949 Big 8 baseball team from Bernice won the championship at Fraser Field in Ruston, Louisiana, where this photograph was taken of the team immediately after the winning game. Shown from left to right are (first row) unidentified, Paul Salley, Joe Green, Bobby Joe Till (bat boy), Luther Lois Farrar, Charles Salley, and unidentified; (second row) Calvin Tanner, Lamar Heard, C.R. Jarmon, DeWell Jeffcoat, Glenn Post Jr. (manager), James Carroll Farrar, Joe Warren Farrar, and Johnny Bledsoe; (third row) Shelby Tucker, Henry Albritton, J.C. Tucker, Dr. Wick Lawrence, Jack O'Bannon, Billy Till, Sam Willis O'Bannon, ? McDonald, Dendy Elliott, Preston Copeland, Billy Ross O'Bannon, and Alton Bradley. (Courtesy Bernice Historical Society.)

These are the 1950 Big 8 league champions. Shown are, from left to right, (first row) Henry Albritton, Johnnie Emmons, Dendy Elliott, Johnny Bledsoe, Elliott Burson, Joe Farrar, Bobby Elkins, and Billy Till; (second row) Alton Bradley, Joe Green, Jack O'Bannon, Preston Copeland, Glenn Post, Ben Carroll, Calvin Tanner, Harry Cunningham, Thomas L. "Lefty" Smith, Herbert Cook, and Al Nicosia. (Courtesy Bernice Historical Society.)

The occasional singing school was one form of entertainment during the early 1900s in rural Union Parish. They were usually sponsored by the local church and were attended by all who could carry a tune and some who could not. The one pictured here was held in Pisgah in August 1911. Addie Thaxton Pryor is fifth from right in the third row, and her sister Emma Thaxton Faulkner is second from right in the second row. Teacher J. Dee Carroll is at the left in the second row. (Author's collection.)

Located in Shiloh, Buckley School served the area for many years, even after most had consolidated. The parents did not want their children to have to travel the two or three miles to attend the Bernice School. (Courtesy Cathy Buckley.)

Shiloh School for black children was built in 1918. Jim Buckley sold an acre to concerned parents who did not want their children to have to walk to another school miles away. The parents got money for the construction by raising and selling cotton. The lumber was cut from land owned by the Friendship Baptist Church, which turned the cleared land into a church cemetery. The schoolhouse was abandoned in the 1940s. (Courtesy Jean Jones.)

The First Baptist Church was chartered in 1902 with William Cooksey serving as the first pastor. The first services were held in a small building on East Main Street in Bernice. Later, they were held in a frame school building before the first church building (pictured here) was built. (Courtesy Bernice Historical Society.)

The Methodist Church was organized in 1901 and constructed this building in 1903. The Arkansas Southern Railroad donated lots 13 and 14 to the Methodist Episcopal Church South for the building of the church. The first pastor was W.T. Woodard. The original structure has been improved over the years. (Courtesy Bernice Historical Society.)

The Alabama Methodist Church is located near the Claiborne Parish line just west of Bernice in the community of Weldon. Construction of the church began in the fall of 1895. R.P. Powell, the pastor of the church, and J.H. Harper were the leading carpenters. Most of the male members also labored on the building. Heart pine was used for the building, with cypress shingles rived to cover the roof. The original handmade pews, benches, and other furniture are still in the sanctuary. The building has not been used since the 1960s but stands as a true historic landmark in Union Parish. (Courtesy Bernice Historical Society.)

This is the second Shiloh Baptist Church building. When the church was established on March 30, 1849, it was called Shiloh Baptist Church of Christ. Tradition says the first structure for Shiloh Baptist Church was of logs. In 1852, Micajah Little donated five acres of land for the church and cemetery. A second structure was built and used until it burned on June 1, 1937. (Courtesy Cathy Buckley.)

After the second church building burned at Shiloh, a new building was constructed and dedicated in 1938. This is a frame structure that has been bricked, upgraded over the years, and is still in use today. (Courtesy Cathy Buckley.)

Bernice Hotel was operated by Linnie Slaughter, whose husband, Thomas L. Slaughter, was a laborer at the Henderson sawmill. The hotel offered workers at the sawmill a place to stay and good meals, all for a modest fee of course. (Courtesy Bernice Historical Society.)

The home of James M. and Mary E. Smith Odom was built by Teanor Salley in about 1895. The family members shown are Mr. and Mrs. Odom, their daughter Euphus L., son Randel C., along with Mrs. Odom's sons William W. and Henry J. Bennett and their wives, Loula and Donna, children from her first marriage to Andrew Jackson Bennett, who died in 1884. (Author's collection.)

Photographer John Berry Adcock's home is shown with Joseph C. Rockett and his daughter Homie in the carriage in front of the house. J.B. Adcock not only made photographs in his studio at home, but also traveled for miles taking photographs of families in the area. At some point his home burned, thereby destroying the treasure of original plates of his many years of work. (Author's collection.)

Sweet Onion was the name R.T. Moore gave to the home he built just after the Civil War. It was built of logs in the dogtrot style with chimneys at both ends. The walls, ceiling, and floors are made of heart pine. The home has passed through several owners over the years and is presently owned by Leroy and Rebecca Stenzel. (Courtesy Bernice Historical Society.)

This one-room cabin, located near Bernice, was built about 1865 of hand-hewn virgin pine logs dovetailed at the corners. All the lumber used in the cabin was fastened with wooden pegs. The shingles for the roof were rived from cypress. There was no glass in the windows; instead, they had wooden shutters that were closed in bad weather. Robert McCuller bought the cabin and 95 acres of land from Marion C. Walker on May 3, 1919. It has since been known as McCuller's cabin. The McCuller family lived in the cabin until 1954. (Courtesy Benice Historical Society.)

This shop was located in the community of Pisgah in about 1900. The small boy pictured second from the left is Kelton Thaxton. Shops such as this one maintained area farmers' plows, wagons, and guns and constructed caskets in times of need. (Courtesy Dr. Robert L. Barrett.)

Wagonloads of cotton are lined up waiting to be unloaded at J.W. Lee's gin on his farm near Shiloh around 1908. After the cotton was ginned, it was sold and transported to warehouses located at the Shiloh landing for transport by steamboat to market. Steamboats could only travel Bayou Cornie in the spring during high water. (Courtesy Mattie Lou Lester and the Council on Aging.)

Dr. Clyde Calhoun Colvin was born on August 23, 1884, in the community of Culbertson. He graduated medical school in 1909 and practiced medicine in Tannehill near Winfield before moving to Bernice in the early 1920s. He established his office in the E.B. Robinson building. In 1927, he moved to the Masonic Building along with dentist Dr. M. Wick Laurence Sr. He remained there until construction of the Colvin and Reeves Clinic and Hospital was completed in 1950. Dr. Colvin retired after 50 years of practice in 1956. (Courtesy Spearsville Photo Gallery.)

Confederate veterans from the Shiloh area shown in this photograph are attending a Civil War reunion, probably in Little Rock, Arkansas. They are, from left to right, Nathan Tabor, R.J. Tabor, J. Hughes, E. Weldon, B. Booles, A. Fuller, J. Hamilton, J. Heard, B. Lynch, unidentified, A. Autrey, P. Heard, J. Digby, and T. Breed. (Courtesy Cathy Buckley.)

All too often, this scene took place throughout Union Parish during the war years of 1942–1945. This Rock Island railcar served as the final ride to Bernice in 1944 for fallen hero Odis Fomby as he is carried to his final resting place by the honor guard. He was laid to rest in Pisgah Cemetery with full military honors. (Courtesy Bernice Depot Museum.)

Three

MARION AND
EASTERN UNION PARISH

This panoramic view shows the bustling town of Marion as it appeared in 1949. Marion became a resting point for immigrants from Alabama, Georgia, and Mississippi who had arrived at the Alabama landing by steamboat. Instead of moving on into Union Parish, many put down their roots there. Marion was named for the county they had called home back in Alabama, which in turn was named for Capt. Francis Marion, who was a hero of the Revolutionary War. For years until the advent of the railroad, Marion was one of the fastest growing towns in Union Parish. (Courtesy Town of Marion.)

Built of heart pine and cypress by a gifted slave named John Thomas, this house was completed in the spring of 1852. The Reverend Elias George, the owner of the house, had moved his family from Marion, Alabama, to Louisiana in 1848 when he captained a caravan of some 50 covered wagons plus numerous other surreys, carts, and men on horseback to the promised "land of paradise" in Louisiana. The house is called the Hopkins house for Mary Hopkins, who was the last to occupy the house. Hopkins died in 1975 at the age of 84. (Author's collection.)

The Crow Motor Company, a Ford dealership, opened on the corner of Main Street and the Huttig Highway in downtown Marion in 1925. It was owned and operated by William E. Crow, who is shown along with his wife, the former Katie Sehon. According to the family, the dealership burned in about 1930. (Courtesy Dewitt Crow.)

Post Garage was owned and operated by Glen F. Post Sr. By the early 1920s, the blacksmith and garage became the first automobile dealership in Marion. The employees are posed in front of new Ford cars on sale at the company. Glen Post is standing third from the left, and on his left is Egan Kenley, the manager and mechanic. Post also carried the mail for the US Postal Service, which required that postal employees could not own a business and hold a position with the service. Post was given the option of resigning his position or disposing of his business interests. He chose the latter. (Courtesy David Post.)

A basketball game is being played in Marion during the 1920s. It looks like one player is shooting a free throw—but what are the others doing? Of course in those days, they jumped center after every score. If a team had a tall player who could get the tip each time, its chance of winning the game was great. (Courtesy Marion Town Hall.)

This tram train was owned by Union Sawmill Company. Pictured in the foreground is a son of Sam Smith—either Minor or Ben. The Union Sawmill Company was organized in 1902 and was located three miles above the Arkansas line near Huttig. The company's tramline ran from the mill south through Litroe, Dean, Haile, Spencer, and on to Sterlington. Along the line, lumber camps were set up as they harvested timber in the area. This railroad was later bought by Missouri Pacific Railroad Company. (Courtesy Gloria Love Garland.)

During the late 1800s and early 1900s, lumber companies, such as Union and Summit, sent agents throughout Union Parish to buy timber. After a tract was bought and right-of-way obtained, the company would build a tramline to the timber and set up a logging camp to harvest it. Shotgun-type buildings were loaded on boxcars, transported to the site, unloaded by crane, and set up for the employees and their families to live in. After the timber was "cut out," the buildings were loaded back on boxcars and carried to the next location. This camp was called camp No. 5 and was located near Linville. (Courtesy Gloria Love Garland.)

Throughout Union Parish in the late 1800s and early 1900s, trams were built from the sawmill site to the timber that was to be harvested. Camps were set up at the end of the line where the logging operation took place. Logs were snaked out of the woods with teams of oxen or mules and loaded onto box cars by crane for transport to the mill. This photograph is of one of the crews and engines used. The tall man in the center is Charles C. Anderson, the foreman of the crew. (Courtesy Jeffy and Vicki Cole.)

Teams of oxen were utilized by logging crews throughout Union Parish in the early 1900s. These powerful animals were the most efficient method of getting logs to the loading sets at the time. Pictured with their team of oxen, this logging crew consists of, from left to right, Dave Russell, Porter Taunton (driver), Hue Cole, and Mack King in the back. (Courtesy Gloria Love Garland.)

These woodsmen armed with crosscut saws are ready for a day's work in the pine woods west of Linville. By 1910 when this photograph was taken, the demand for lumber changed the mindset of landowners in the area. In the past, trees were considered a nuisance and had to be destroyed by having what was known as "log rollings" to clear land for farming. After the advent of the railroad, lumber could be transported efficiently to markets outside the parish, and timber became an asset to landowners. (Courtesy Gloria Love Garland.)

These two teams of mules are pulling Lindsey wagons loaded with pine logs. The team on the left is driven by Cliff Taunton. Raymond Day is riding on the logs, and Ollie Day is driving the team on the right. (Courtesy Gloria Love Garland.)

This steam-driven hay baler was located on the Jim Love farm in about 1910. This invention not only saved space when storing hay because it compressed it into bales instead of having to store the hay loose in the loft of the barn, but it also made the hay easier to handle. (Courtesy Gloria Love Garland.)

The W. Blake Haile and Sons sawmill operated during the 1940s near Haile. Mills such as this one were the source of lumber for communities throughout Union Parish. The lumber from private mills was used locally while company mills shipped large quantities of lumber by rail. (Courtesy Jimmy Dean.)

On August 5, 1933, Matthew Wood, No. 1440 Civilian Conservation Corps (CCC) Camp, was dedicated near Marion. The CCC was a public works relief program that operated from 1933 to 1942 as part of the New Deal of Pres. Franklin D. Roosevelt. Its purpose was to allow unemployed unmarried men between the ages 18 to 25 the opportunity to serve for six months to provide

financial relief to their families. Men from throughout Union Parish signed up to serve at the camp. Van Cole, of Spearsville, who signed up on January 6, 1934, was one of these men. Reserve officers from the US Army were in charge of the camp. (Courtesy Jeffy & Vicki Cole.)

Pictured here is the CCC Camp No. 1440 baseball team. Unfortunately, only two of the players' names are known. Author Washam from Lillie is first on the left in the first row and Van Cole from Spearsville is third from left in the first row. (Courtesy of Eunice Cole.)

During the 1920s, the family farms in Union Parish were virtually self-supporting. The basic foods that made up the diet of the population were grown on the farm, and other essentials were made from products on the farm. Lye soap was commonly made from the fat of hogs at hog-killing time in the fall after the first frost. Sugarcane was harvested, cooked down, and turned into molasses, as demonstrated in this photograph taken on the Jimmy Love farm near Linville in 1915. Jimmy is the man on the right with the beard. (Courtesy Jimmy Dean.)

After completing a photography course in New York, Royal Oliver Love returned to his home in Union Parish to establish a business making photographs. He hired Bob Williamson, a local carpenter, to construct a mobile studio. The wagon was completed and loaded with the equipment, supplies, and chemicals needed in a studio. The wagon worked fine until it started down the D'Loutre hill. His load shifted, and the wagon turned over, scattering his supplies down the hill and into the woods. Undeterred, Oliver gathered his supplies and returned home to make adjustments in loading the wagon. He set out again, and made it to Farmerville to start his professional career as a photographer. (Courtesy Gloria Garland.)

Oliver Love traveled throughout eastern Union Parish plying his photography trade. He is shown in 1915 with his young son Lucine behind the wheel of his first car, which he bought in 1911. The steering wheel is on the right. (Courtesy Gloria Love Garland.)

Kleber S. Thompson built this home in Marion in the early 1930s. He owned and operated Thompson's general store in Marion. Hugh Barron built a general store across the street from the Crow Motor Company lot in the late 1930s. Hugh's brother, Chester Barron ran the store and lived in an upstairs apartment over the store. He was in direct competition with Kleber S. Thompson, who just happened to be on the draft board for the armed service. To rid himself of the competition, he had Chester drafted into the Army in 1942. Kleber Thompson's daughter is the mother of Kix Brooks, of the famed country-singing duo Brooks and Dunn. (Author's collection.)

In 1903, Samuel Lorenzo Haile donated land for a new railroad to come through the area that was to become Haile with two conditions attached to the donation. The first was that a depot would be built on the land, and the other was that the new town be named Haile. On November 27, 1905, the town of Haile was surveyed and mapped by W.E. Atkinson. (Courtesy Gloria Love Garland.)

Brown's store in Haile was built in 1930 and torn down in 1986. The last post office in Haile, which closed in 1970, was located in this store. Most post offices were located in the local stores in earlier times, but by the 1960s, this was not the case—it was the exception. (Courtesy Jimmy Dean.)

After land was donated to entice the railroad through Haile, the tracks were laid and a depot established there in 1904. The depot (seen in the background at right) closed in 1933, but the trains continued to travel through Haile after Missouri Pacific upgraded the system in 1945–1960. By 1980, the rail system was in disrepair. Delta Southern bought the railroad to transport wood products. The railroad was abandoned in 1993 and the tracks removed. (Courtesy Jimmy Dean.)

The records from *Paxton's History of Baptists in Louisiana* indicates that Liberty Baptist Church near Linville was formed in the late 1840s. All Missionary Baptist churches joined the Concord Association soon after they formed and Liberty joined in 1850. Elias George, who came to Union Parish from Perry County, Alabama, in 1850, was the first known pastor. Liberty was the only Baptist church on the east side of Union Parish for many years. In 1850, Lewis Lanair donated two acres of land for a new building to replace the first building, which was located one quarter mile south of the new location. The cemetery was established in 1853. Several church buildings have been built and replaced over the years. The present building was dedicated April 1, 1956. The story was told that one of the church buildings fell off its foundation during a service one Sunday morning and as a man dove out one of the windows, the window sash came crashing down, catching him by the feet. As he hung dangling from the window he was heard praying, "Save me Lord! The Devil's got a holt to me!" (Courtesy Gloria Love Garland.)

The Union Methodist Church building was constructed in 1943 from lumber from the Union School at Tiger Bend, which had been closed. It was actually built by women in the community, including Ruby Green Savage and Velma Edwards Platt. The ladies would meet once a week to pull nails from the salvaged lumber. Ruby Green Savage and Bob and Ethel Platt are standing in the doorway to the church. (Courtesy Terry Lee Pratt.)

This photograph shows Marion's wood-framed high school building. When it met its demise by fire, it was replaced with a brick structure. Smaller schools in the area began closing, and the students transferred after Marion High was established. (Courtesy Town of Marion.)

The newly instituted public school system in Union Parish brought about innovations. Instead of having to walk as far as five miles to the country school of the past, the students at the new Marion High School were transported by bus. The first such so-called bus is shown decked out in its full regalia and loaded with students. The new high school building is seen in the background. (Courtesy Gloria Love Garland.)

Marion won the Class B championship in 1939. The mascot in front is Phillips. Coach Causey is pictured in back. Players include, from left to right, (first row) Jarmon, Gilbert, Crow, Phillips, Mike, and Crow; (second row) Vestal, Miller, Smith, Crow, Ward, and Post. (Courtesy Town of Marion.)

Members of the 1943–1944 Marion women's basketball team are, from left to right, (first row) Ernestine Bowen, Jean Gibson, Hilda Ellen Landers, Thelma Miller, and Clara Duke; (second row) Helen Rose Crow, Virginia Green, Patricia Tucker, Frances Burson, Gertrude Thurman, and Mary Grace Thompson. (Courtesy Town of Marion.)

The members of the 1949–1950 Marion High School band are, from left to right, (first row) Beverly Crow, Ann Melton, Sue Melton, Murphy Oliver, Wayne Causey, Helen Tucker, James Green, DeWitt Platt, Laddie McVicker, Joe Tucker, Toby Medlin, Everett Eugene Reppond, Roy Arrant, George Sehon, and unidentified; (second row) Gayle Brasher, Sue Edwards, Jerry Daniels, unidentified, Viva Ann Whelis, Eloise McKinnie, Mary Margaret Griggs, Charles Farrar, James Rockett, Dorothy Jean Gilbert, Ardis Lee Phillips, three unidentified, and Mr. Welch; (third row) Malcolm McVicker, Mary Jo Andrews, Frenchie Odom, Mary Alma Graves, Martha Jean England, Clyde Brashier, Peggy Dell Gilbert, Geraldine McKinnie, Jo Ann Gilbert, JoAnna Rockett, Jane Jarmon, Morris Gilmore, and Roy Post. (Courtesy Town of Marion.)

Another of the initial public schools in Union Parish, Sadie School was located in the community of Sadie in northeast portion of Union Parish. Althoght Miss Eunice Cole began her long teaching career at Wilhite, she taught at Sadie before transferring to Spearsville. (Courtesy Union Parish Library.)

The Ouachita Public School was another of the first public schools established in Union Parish when the system was initiated in 1909. This school in the southeast section of Union Parish only offered grades through the seventh. (Courtesy Union Parish Library.)

The Spencer Public School was among the original public schools established after the public school system was initiated. Students would come from four to five miles away to attend school. Some were fortunate enough to ride by wagon, horse, or mule, but most walked. (Courtesy Union Parish Library.)

The China Grove School was located some four miles southwest of Haile. It served the area until it was consolidated with Linville High in 1923. Viola Harrell is said to have taught at the school. Students brought their lunches to school each day, many in syrup buckets. (Courtesy Gloria Love Garland.)

This Linville High School building was constructed shortly before 1909 when the new public school system began. John R. Love is the driver of the lead wagon. Those identified in the photograph are Lee Phillips, Gus Joiner, Sam Love, Sally Savage, Fannie Smith, Mattie Smith, and Lillian Turner. (Courtesy Gloria Love Garland.)

Located at Tiger Bend near Marion, the Union School was across the road from the home of William Ernest and Ruby Green Savage. It was another of the schools created when the public school system began in 1909. It was closed, and the children transferred to Marion High School in 1943. (Courtesy Terry Lee Pratt.)

Linville High School offered much to the students in the area. Many smaller schools in the area closed over time, and the students transferred to Linville. In this shot of the members of the 1917 Linville High School brass band, only the names of the first three in the front row are known. They are Everett Love, Lifford Allen, and Percy Turner. (Courtesy Gloria Love Garland.)

Springfield School was located in Dean next to Dean Baptist Church between Marion and Linville. It was consolidated with Linville public school in about 1950. The students attending the school in 1903 are (first row) M.H. Pardue, Johnnie Reppond, Charlie Reppond, Mack Pace, Grover Reppond, B.L. Reppond, Robert Abscent, and Duff Smith; (second row) Emma Edwards, Beulah Reppond, Viola Edwards, Tom Reppond, Sally Smith, Maud Turner, John P. Reppond, Luther Reppond, Eulah Reppond, Jesse Reppond, Alma Abscent, and Dock Smith; (third row) Hugh Cole, Dee G. Russell, Oscar Pace, Calvin Pardue, Etta Reppond, Hattie Pilgreen, Dora Reppond, Katie Abscent, George Reppond, and John W. Abscent; (fourth row) Charlie Langford, Mollie Turner, Dixie Russell, Mary Pilgreen, Ella Smith, Lou Smith Turner, Lula Reppond, Ethel Reppond, Rev. William Smith, Agnes Smith, Mary Reppond, and Susie Abscent. The man in back is Professor Griffin. (Courtesy Jon McKinnie.)

The Linville High School classroom building was constructed in 1930 and was used until 1948 when a new structure replaced it. A cafeteria-auditorium combination was part of the new construction. (Courtesy Gloria Love Garland.)

In 1938, Linville High School sported a rhythm band in full regalia led by their teacher Maurene Breazeal, who had transferred to Linville High from the school at Tugwell City. (Courtesy Maurene Breazeal Barron.)

Students attending Haile High School in the 1946–1947 school year are, from left to right, (first row) Clifton Snell, Peggy Gilmore, John Shadic, Joy Lynn Thomas, Mary Ford, Edwina Pace, ? Chamblis, Jimmy McGlothin, Charlie Johnson, Agnes Howard, and Greta Waller; (second row) Jimmy Wayne Smith, James Snell, Viola Thomas, Robert Earl Snell, Jerry Beckley, Blondell Guinn, Della Mae Snell, Cecil Shadic, Clifton Roberson, and John Jeff Hollis; (third row) C.W. Wheeler, Jerry Lee Shadic, Peggy Roberson, Tommy Gilmore, Robert Dean, Jimmy Dean, Billy Chamblis, Emily Lee Snell, Johnny Thomas, Adolphus Snell, Charlie Barr, and Vernon Ray; (fourth row) ? Carroll (grades one–three teacher), J.M. Waldrop (principal), and Edna Lankford (cook). (Courtesy Jimmy Dean.)

Through the efforts of former Arkansas governor George Washington Donaghey, who was born near Marion, this monument was established on the border of Union County, Arkansas, and Union Parish, Louisiana, in 1931. Intricate carvings denote the different modes of transportation from 1831 until 1931. It also makes reference to Huey P. Long, whose educational programs in Louisiana were admired by Governor Donaghey. Over the years, vandals all but destroyed the monument. In 1975, Rep. Louise Johnson obtained passage of a law to refurbish the monument, which was not completed until 2009. (Author's collection.)

Union Sawmill located in Huttig, Arkansas, constructed a railroad from Huttig to Spencer to transport logs from the area to its mill. In the 1990s, Delta Southern bought the line and transported chips to Olin's paper mill in West Monroe for Plum Creek. The rail system by this point was so badly in need of repair that mishaps were almost a daily occurrence and speed was limited to five miles per hour. Crews followed the train to put it back in place in the event it left the tracks. The last train wreck occurred a mile south of Haile along Highway 143. The last train to make the run is pictured above. The tracks were abandoned in 1993 and removed in 1999. (Courtesy Jimmy Dean.)

The O.K. Allen Bridge was dedicated by Huey Long in 1932. It was part of Huey Long's highway-and-bridge-building program but was completed under O.K. Allen's administration after Long had resigned to run for the senate. In 2009, a new bridge was completed, which is located just north of the O.K. Allen Bridge. The old bridge was demolished that same year. (Author's collection.)

Tom Douglas was born into slavery in 1847 to Burwell B. Thomas, of Marion. In an interview in 1936, Douglas said, "When we was 'mancipated in '65 our master took us outside the gate across the road and told us we was freed. 'You are free to work for anybody you want to.' We set there a while then we went whare ol' master was and he tol' us if we wanted to stay wid' him and finish the crop he would provide our victuals and clothes. The next year we worked for him on halves and did so for four or five years." Of hundreds of former slaves interviewed in the 1930s, only Douglas said he was better off then than he was in slave days. He was successful, owning land and money in the bank. The others interviewed claimed they were better off during slavery. They claimed that during slavery, although they were beaten at times, they were well fed and clothed and all they had to do was work—"we didn't mind work." Sarah was born a slave in Alabama. Sarah and Tom married in about 1870. (Courtesy George Douglas.)

Four

SPEARSVILLE AND
NORTHWESTERN UNION PARISH

Taken in 1953, this aerial photograph of Spearsville looking east shows Barron's store in the upper center. Just below to the right is the Dennis Lockwood store, the abandoned store of Minor Ogden and barbershop of William Ogden, and the third building is Clyde Barron's service station. The two-story building to the lower left is the Masonic lodge. In front of it is Glover Rockett's service station. Behind and to the left of Barron's store is the cotton gin, and behind it is the Dr. Dudley house. In the upper right is Spearsville High School. The Victor Cole home is at the bottom left. Shortly after this photograph was taken, the Lockwood and Ogden stores were destroyed by fire and never rebuilt. (Courtesy Glenn Barron.)

This cotton gin in Spearsville was built and operated by William L. Jinks and owned by Robert "Lum" Henderson. Henderson sold it to S.J. Berry Abbett, who in turn sold it to G.E. Lindsey, of Bernice, on May 27, 1927. Many men sported a hook instead of a hand because of the gin. (Author's collection.)

With the coming of the automobile, Dan Senn, financed by Dr. O.C. O'Neal, built the first service station in Spearsville in 1921. The next year, it burned down but was rebuilt and sold to Arkie Pryor, who operated the station until 1945 when he sold it to first cousins George Harmon and Curtis Smith. Arkie Pryor, shown in front of the station, operated the first street lighting system in the town utilizing a gas generator in his station. The generator kept the town lit until about 10:00 p.m. when Pryor would announce, "Okay folks it's time to go home!" After giving folks time to leave town, he would kill the generator, and the town went dark. (Courtesy Dr. Robert L. Barrett.)

This photograph taken in the 1940s depicts Barron's general store in the center. Lindsey's cotton gin is seen to the left of the store. Smith & Rockett's store can be seen on the right. At the left in front of Barron's store is the town's old water well covered with a low, flat roof. During the 1930s, this was the hitching area for mules and wagons. Also, drinking gourds hung at either end of the well—one for whites and one for blacks. (Author's collection.)

85

Berry Abbett's store in Spearsville is pictured about 1924. Those shown are, from left to right, Berry's wife Delta, Shep Welch, Emma Long, unidentified, and Berry Abbett. The heirs of Joseph R. Goyne sold the store and other property to Abbett in 1904 and he remained a major Spearsville property owner until his retirement in the 1940s. (Courtesy of John Rhodes.)

Robert "Lum" Henderson bought this store from Cull Elliott in 1920 when the Elliotts moved to Leola, Arkansas. Lum is at left, Conrad is sitting on the floor, with Robbie Lee standing next to him, and Clarence Breazeal, who worked for Lum, is standing at right. (Author's collection.)

Joseph and Elizabeth Cole bought the property of her brother John C. Cole, which was sold for taxes at a sheriff's sale in 1890. This property included a store in Spearsville. A few years later, they built a new store across the road from the old one. During the 1920s, the store was owned by Leroy Futch, Lawrence Carroll, and Cliff Carroll, shown from left to right. Years later, S.J. Berry Abbett bought the store from the Carrolls. (Courtesy Carroll family.)

Joseph Elton Rockett bought the Spears store from W.S. Spears on January 24, 1920. Spears had inherited it from his father, Dr. Joe Brooks Spears, son of Alexander Spears, who is given credit for founding the town. After many years of operating the store, he sold it to Hugh Rockett and Woody Smith, who in turn sold to Grady Rockett. Grady Rockett sold out to Clyde McDougald, who later sold to Dennis Lockwood who owned the store when it burned in the spring of 1953. Joseph's wife, Ozella Reagan Rockett, and their daughter, Elizabeth, are shown here. (Courtesy Wayne Barrett.)

The *Helen Vaughn* was a major transporter of goods from Cobb's landing to Monroe and points in between during her existence in the 1880s. She was owned and operated by Captain H.W. Vaughn and later by Harry Meek Williams. At 25 feet, she was wider than most boats that served landings on the D'Arbonne and Cornie Bayous. In 1894 she made 11 trips between Cobb's landing, located at the mouth of Ten Mile Creek, and Monroe. The bayous are strewn with the wreckage of steamboats; shipping goods on the boats put the goods at peril, but there was little alternative in the days before the railroad. In March 1895, the *Helen Vaughn* caught fire, supposedly from sparks from her smoke stack, and burned at Whites Ferry near the mouth of D'Arbonne along with 450 bales of cotton from Shiloh landing and Stein's Bluff. (Courtesy of Patricia Freeman.)

Before the turn of the 20th century, Abraham Henderson and his wife, the former Mary V. Arrington, built this home in Spearsville. The Hendersons moved to Junction City, Arkansas, some years later and built another home in its image. Thad Grace bought the home from the Hendersons and eventually sold it to Paul A. Griffon. After the Griffons abandoned the home and moved into a new one, the old house fell into disrepair. After several years it accidentally caught fire and burned. Joe and Sue Futch bought the charred remains, cleared the lot, and built a new home in its stead. (Courtesy of Patricia Freeman.)

This home was built in the dogtrot style in 1865 by John Hardin Brazeal. Hosea Bright Breazeal bought the home shortly thereafter. The home was constructed of hand-hewed logs fitted with full dovetails at the corners. Hand-hewed rafters were secured with wooden pegs. The two chimneys of the house were constructed of iron ore rock secured with mud mortar. The farm equipment was made onsite and included a handmade hay baler made completely of wood. A rail fence lined the road as it approached the house, which was located a quarter mile from the main road. Sadly, after serving the Breazeal family for over 140 years, it was torn down in about 2006. (Author's collection.)

In the early 1900s, Dr. Varner Edward Dudley and his wife, the former Sarah Louise Henderson, built a house in Spearsville. Dr. Dudley was burning the crate that their new stove had been shipped in, and a spark ignited the cedar shingles on the roof, causing the house to burn to the ground. In 1910, Dr. Dudley hired Teanor Sally to build another house for his family like the one Salley had built in Bernice for James M. Odom in the Victorian style. This house still stands and is occupied today. (Author's collection.)

In December 1864, Dr. John Arrington and Sarah Amanda Barron were married in Union Parish and shortly thereafter built the house pictured above. Although it is a log house, it has been covered over the years with so-called modern material. In about 1880, the Arringtons moved to Corney Lake in Claiborne Parish. Many families have lived there after the Arringtons. Sarah's sister and her husband, John Sidney Post, owned the house and sold it to George and Dora Cole in 1906. They established the first telephone exchange in Spearsville in the house. After the Coles came the families of Joshua Lambert and Murphy Crow. Murphy served as principal at Spearville High School from 1932 until 1935. William Paul Crow was born in the house in December 1933. The last family to live in the house was the Anderson Lee Barron family. Anderson Lee died in the house in April 1959. Sadly, the house has gone to decay. (Author's collection.)

By 1870, schooling came to the forefront at Spearsville under the leadership of W.L. Hodge, and in 1891, his school evolved into Everett Institute when the Everett Association voted to sponsor the school. A committee from the association asked for bids from different locations in the area, and Spearsville was chosen, as it offered the best assets. Led by Rev. J.V.B. Waldrop, funds were raised for the construction. A building was erected to accommodate 225 students, and J.R. Thomas was hired as principal. Some of the teachers were Mr. Stringer, Mr. Thorne, Mrs. Tom Terral, Mrs. Ponder, Zula Breazeal, Sudie Mae Carroll, Dora Cole, and Maude Carroll, who taught music. The school was donated to the public school system when it was initiated in 1909. (Author's collection.)

The students attending Spearsville Public School in 1909, its first year of existence, include, from left to right, (first row) Etta Burton, Olivia Cole, ? Bryan, Clara Wallace, two unidentified, Marie Cole, two unidentified, John Heard Jr., Clarence Stone, unidentified, Charlie Wallace, Clarence Breazeal, Edwin Elliott, and unidentified; (second row) unidentified, Beth Pryor, Bertha Heard, Conrad Henderson, two unidentified, Milton Buckley, Lois Pickens, Zula Breazeal, Rosa Pickens, Arkie Pryor, Nannie Heard, Emma Owens, Tom Elliott, and two unidentified; (third row) Lucille Carroll, Fred Grace, Dudie Mae Carroll, Emmett Everett, David Burnside, Stanley Cherry, Lee Caulk, Pellium Williams, Lillian Pryor, Janie Cherry, Sallie Pickens, and Vera Cole. (Author's collection.)

As more and more area schools closed and students transferred to the public high school at Spearsville, there was a demand for more classrooms. The result was this two-story building completed in 1921. Soon thereafter, all the local schools closed and sent their students to Spearsville. (Courtesy Wayne Barrett.)

{1915}
Rules For Teachers

1. YOU WILL NOT MARRY DURING THE TERM OF YOUR CONTRACT.

2. YOU ARE NOT TO KEEP COMPANY WITH MEN.

3. YOU MUST BE HOME BETWEEN THE HOURS OF 8 P.M. AND 6 A.M. UNLESS ATTENDING A SCHOOL FUNCTION.

4. YOU MAY NOT LOITER DOWNTOWN IN ICE CREAM STORES.

5. YOU MAY NOT TRAVEL BEYOND THE CITY LIMITS UNLESS YOU HAVE THE PERMISSION OF THE CHAIRMAN OF THE BOARD.

6. YOU MAY NOT RIDE IN A CARRIAGE OR AUTOMOBILE WITH ANY MAN UNLESS HE IS YOUR FATHER OR BROTHER.

7. YOU MAY NOT SMOKE CIGARETTES.

8. YOU MAY NOT DRESS IN BRIGHT COLORS.

9. YOU MAY UNDER NO CIRCUMSTANCES DYE YOUR HAIR.

10. YOU MUST WEAR AT LEAST TWO PETTICOATS.

11. YOUR DRESSES MUST NOT BE ANY SHORTER THAN TWO INCHES ABOVE THE ANKLE.

12. TO KEEP THE SCHOOL ROOM NEAT AND CLEAN, YOU MUST: SWEEP THE FLOOR AT LEAST ONCE DAILY. SCRUB THE FLOOR AT LEAST ONCE A WEEK WITH HOT, SOAPY WATER. CLEAN THE BLACKBOARDS AT LEAST ONCE A DAY AND START THE FIRE AT 7 A.M. SO THE ROOM WILL BE WARM BY 8 A.M.

Strict were the rules required of teachers in the early years of the public school system. Married women were thought to have responsibilities at home, and teaching was to be done by single women—or by single and married men. These rules seem extreme in today's liberal society but were the norm in those days. (Courtesy Billy Henderson.)

Varner E. Dudley taught school at Zion Hill in about 1900 before becoming the renowned doctor of Spearsville. For 39 years, he practiced medicine in Spearsville and was known far and wide for his medical ability and dedication. Once, after diagnosing appendicitis in a female patient, he sent her to Shreveport for an operation along with a note to the operating physician telling him that the patient's appendix was on the left side. Ignoring the note, the physician operated on the right side and found no appendix. He had to perform a second operation to remove the infected organ. Dr. Dudley was held in high esteem with that surgeon from then on. (Courtesy Spearsville Photo Gallery & Museum.)

The Beech Grove Methodist Church can be seen in the background of this photograph. Students at Beech Grove school shown are, from left to right, (first row) Archie Dison, Cecil Pate, Dalton Taylor, Chester Taylor, Troy Smith, John Dison, Jake Dison, Ray Taylor, Tommy Taylor, Willie Warner Barron, Donald Hollis, Flavel Hollis, Josh Hollis, Garland Linder, Brady Black, Lester Smith, Elton Dettenheim, John Thomas, Lavelle Brantley, Aubrey Taylor, and Melvin Grissom; (second row) Alto Smith, Anna Dison, Myrtis Smith, Lee Linder, Zola Mae Grissom, Audrey Butler, Thelma Linder, Bessie Henderson, Ellene Barron, Opal Barron, Selma Dison, Eva Dison, Robbie Butler, Narvie Taylor, Willie Dison, Clara Dison, Carrie Dison, Mildred Dettenheim, Audrey Taylor, Beatrice Henderson, Mildred Grissom, Carrie Hollis, Vera Hollis, and Maude Hollis; (third row) Curtis Bryam, Tom Hollis, Garland Thomas, John Lamyre Barron, Varner Dison, Ernest Butler, Buddy Smith, Lester Linder, Lonnie Tucker, Lloyd Pratt, Loutie Taylor, Edna Smith, Audrey Smith, Bera Black, Verdell Gunter, Ruby Clark, Louquincy Taylor, Deloris Gunter, Lora Hollis, Lyda Hollis, Inez Raborn, Ethel Hill, Ellie Farrar, and Andrew Thompson; (fourth row) Clifford Tucker, Leon Smith, Proctor Taylor, Carl Taylor, Issac Smith, Clevis Smith, Louie Smith, Otis Smith, Aaron Raborn, Warner Butler, Minor Linder, Brady Thurman, Carl Thomas, Ina Tillman, Etta Black, Eva Raborn, Louizer Hollis, Nettie Henderson, Lillie Barron, Vergie Tillman, Berdell Hollis, Nina Gunter, Lorine Grissom, Susanna Tillman, Maxine Barron, and Irene Raborn. (Courtesy Ethelle Colvin.)

Students at Canaan school in about 1935 are, from left to right, (first row) Wayne Post, Lester Hollis, Shirley Mason, Calvin Vickers, R.S. Burnside, Yvonne Mason, and Lillian Hollis; (second row) Margie Upshaw, David Upshaw, Janice Risinger, Marguerite Vickers, Dorothy Creed, Warner Hollis, Coy Upshaw, and Jack Taylor; (third row) Principal Dennis Duke, Grady Snearly, John M. Creed, Ophelia Manning, Lou Nell Risinger, Audrey Lee Vickers, Gleen Bryan, Charlene Peppers, and Clois Bryan. (Courtesy of the Spearsville Photo Gallery and Museum.)

Camp Creek School began in the early 1900s just below the Camp Creek Baptist Church. Rudolph Farrar served as principal in the early years. The children attending would walk as many as five miles to school each day, bringing their lunches with them in a bucket. (Author's collection.)

Pine Grove School was located about three miles southeast of Laran at the intersection of Jackson Slough–Truxno and Mt. Olive–Conway Roads. The students in the summer of 1900 are (first row) Eva Lockwood, Lillian Lockwood, Era Golsby, Naughvelle Futch, Lee Harrison, Minnie Martin, Winnie Golsby, Edwin Golsby, Lena Futch, Cornelius Futch, Julia Martin, Allen Martin, Pearl Holloway, and William Allen Jones; (second row) Monroe Golsby, Sally McMurrain, John Tom Harrison, Oscar Futch, Ola Futch, Emmett E. Harrison, Vadar Futch, Ed Martin, Nannie Futch, George Futch, Mittie McMurrian, and Molly Bird (teacher); (third row) Steve Lockwood, John Golsby, Mary Alice Harrison, Joe Harrison, Bob Futch, Mae Holloway, Jack Boone, Effie Jean Futch, and Ada Holloway. (Courtesy Terry Lee Pratt.)

New Hope Primitive Baptist Church sponsored a school in 1909. Pictured from left to right are (first row) Louise Rockett, Ottis Rockett, and Eva Taylor; (second row) Bernard Taylor, Thelma Rockett, Margie Rockett, Juanita Taylor, Irene Smith, Ophelia Williams, and Elmer Taylor; (third row) Woody Smith, Elizabeth Ogden, Dallas Wood, Ruth Groves, William Ogden, Ethel Ogden, Robert Summers, and John Lee Smith; (fourth row) Annie Ogden, Harmon Smith, Minnie Summers, Rose Wood, Henry Smith, Ica Webb, Buck Breazeal, Alto Wood, and Minor Taylor. (Courtesy of Lyle Smith.)

The rural school of Mt. Olive drew students from the area of Laran and points south before closing, at which time the students transferred to the public school at Spearsville. At one point, there were over 60 schools similar to Mt. Olive throughout the parish. (Courtesy Spearsville Photo Gallery & Museum.)

Lillie School began in about 1909 and had one of the largest student populations in the parish at its peak. The school building was one of the most attractive and best maintained in the parish. It too closed when consolidation took place and the students transferred to Bernice. (Courtesy Roslyn Johnson.)

The community of Randolph was chosen for the location of one of the first schools established in Union Parish after the public school system was initiated. The students were children of the employees of Summit Lumber Company. Shortly after Summit went bankrupt in 1914, the community dispersed and the school closed. (Courtesy Union Parish Library.)

In about 1965, the Mt. Pisgah Baptist Church was organized. Standing at right is the pastor, Rev. T.L. Green. The deacons (standing) are, from left to right, Earnest Louie, George Reddick, Herman Herts, O.D. Payne, Sam Youngblood, Harrison Douglas, and Ellis Lowe. Seated is Milton Douglas. (Courtesy George Douglas.)

The deaconesses at the newly formed Mt. Pisgah Baptist Church are, from left to right, (first row) Sarah Gray, Lou Ann Payne, Jean Lowe, and Ophelia Lowe; (second row) Rev. T.L. Green, Shirley Herts, and Jane Reddick. (Courtesy George Douglas.)

Members of the Women's Missionary Union (WMU) of the Spearsville Baptist Church in the 1960s include (first row) Jewell Carroll, Mattie Stone, Grace Upshaw, Artie Boatright, Willie Cherry, and Homie Beaird; (second row) Viola Rockett, Louisa Dudley, Gurthrie Spears, Rosa Everett, Etta Bennett, Julia Carroll, Etta Barron, Ethel Barron, Oma Farrar, Ethel Halsey, and Edna Breazeal. (Author's collection.)

Before the public school systems were initiated throughout Louisiana, most schools were sponsored by the local churches. Such was the case with Mt. Union Baptist Church. The church building can be seen in the back and the schoolhouse in front and to the right. Students attending the school are posed in front. (Courtesy Spearsville Photo Gallery & Museum.)

A Baptist Church was organized in June 1848 about four miles east of Spearsville and was designated as Fellowship by its members, who chose Rev. Jupu Tubb as pastor. In 1850, a new church was built in Spearsville on land donated by Daniel Abbott. A new church building was constructed again in 1856, and the name changed to Spearsville Baptist Church of Christ, and again to Spearsville Baptist Church. That building was replaced in 1907 with the one shown above, which was used until it was replaced in 1945 with the one that stands today. Among those pictured are Rev. W.H. Johnson (first row, third from left) and scattered throughout are Dr. V.E. Dudley, J.C. Lambert, P.A. Griffon, Charlie Cherry, Cull Elliott, John Elliott, Lum Henderson, Olivia Cole Pickens, Beth Pryor Harper, Lillian Harper, Vera Cole, Jenny Cobb, Boone Breazeal, Woodford Breazeal, Etta Burton, and Callie Booles Dudley. (Courtesy Eunice Cole.)

Camp Creek Baptist Church was established in the 1860s and continues to serve the community of Camp Creek today. The site was chosen because a spring was located nearby. At the time this building was constructed, the custom was for the men to sit on one side of the church and the women on the other, thus the two doors—one for the men and the other for the women. A portion of the church cemetery can be seen at right. (Author's collection.)

The communities of Lockhart and Antioch each had an early Church of Christ. Bill Risinger was one of the early preachers of the Church of Christ faith. This photograph was taken in about 1915 at the original Church of Christ in Lockhart. Bud Goodson is the man at the left of the doorway holding his daughter Robbie. On the left is Robert Davis holding his daughter Lois. In the middle, the girl holding the purse is Floy Peppers. On either side of her are Allie and Callie Risinger. The tall man in front is Marshall Summers holding his daughter Annie Vell. (Courtesy Brent Patterson.)

Farming was the mainstay in the rural area around Spearsville. The work was hard, but there was time between the planting and the gathering for some relaxation, as demonstrated in this photograph of a band on the Henry Barron farmstead. They are Loy Smith on banjo and Barron brothers Willie on guitar, Guy on fiddle, Lavelle on guitar, and Gurvis on mandolin. There was not a lot of singing, but there was a lot of playing. (Author's collection.)

This logging crew on the job was photographed shortly after the turn of the 20th century probably around the Camp Creek community. Charles Willis Christian is the tall man near the center labeled with the number 1. Aquilla Davis is seated on the logs at right and labeled with the number 2. Seabon Richard Byram is standing at right center labeled with the number 3. (Author's collection.)

In early 1899, Frank Farrar offered Capt. C.C. Henderson right-of-way through his property and land for a depot if he would change his route south to come through his property. A deal had been struck that would have taken the railroad south through Shiloh, but Henderson scrapped the plan and accepted Farrar's offer. The result was devastation for Shiloh but a windfall to what would become Lillie. This photograph of the depot at Lillie was taken in 1909. (Author's collection.)

Reginald Farrar (left) and Fred B. Tisinger are shown in the Lillie depot in 1911. Tisinger was the depot agent, and Farrar was his assistant. Lillie depot was a bustling place in Lillie during the town's early years as goods such as cotton were shipped to market via train and passenger service was offered. (Author's collection.)

John Evens Farrar owned and operated this store in Lillie during the 1930s–1940s. He is shown along with his sister Auby who worked in the store. At the time, this was one of several stores in Lillie offering a variety of goods. (Author's collection.)

During the 1940s, the Rock Island's Doodle Bug made two trips per day from points north to Ruston. The train's whistle could be heard for miles around as it made its final run each day in the quiet of the evening. The Doodle Bug made its last run in the early 1950s. It is pictured at the Lillie depot as Mr. and Mrs. Caraway and their son George board. (Courtesy Janet Bowlin Phillips.)

The Lillie baseball team of 1948 consisted of (first row) Theron Davis holding his son Sidney, Thurman McKnight, Austin Adcock (coach), Buck Rockett, and John M. Creed; (second row) Joe LeBeff, Almer Rockett, James Washam, ? Nash, Dwayne Washam, Lavelle Williams, Graydon Smith, and C.W. Nelson. The boy in front is unidentified. (Courtesy Annette Washam.)

Summit Lumber Company sawmill is shown along with its employees. The mill was located alongside the Arkansas Southern Railroad tracks a few miles south of Junction City, Arkansas. The mill gave rise to a community that became known as Randolph. The mill operated in Randolph from about 1905 until it went into receivership in 1914. In the years following the demise of Summit Lumber Company, Randolph joined the ranks of many other small towns in the parish as a ghost town. (Courtesy Janet Bowlin Phillips.)

This map shows the railway extension to Lockhart and Tugwell City with proposed extensions to Pineville, Timber City, and Monroe. When the Arkansas Southern got into financial trouble and caused the Summit Lumber Company to go bankrupt in 1914, this extension was never completed. (Courtesy David Dawkins.)

The Arkansas Southern Railway locomotive is leaving one of Summit's logging camps headed for the mill at Randolph. Some known locations of Summit logging camps were Lockhart, Beulah, Cherry Ridge, and Pisgah. Notable are the living quarters located on both sides of the tracks, which were hauled on flatcars from location to location and set up for the workers to live in. Upon arriving at a new location, the houses were unloaded by crane and set up before the logging operation could begin. Some of the employees at the camps were (not pictured) Boone Breazeal (log scaler), I.P. Breazeal (commissary clerk), Dr. Perry Tatum (camp doctor), and Garland Bryant (camp cook). Other workers at the camp were Berson Stone, Tom Smith, and a gentleman with the last name Statton, who was from Junction City. (Courtesy Janet Bowlin Phillips.)

Employees of Summit Lumber Company are pictured in this 1913 photograph. That could be J.S. Blackwell, the president of Summit, standing in the doorway of the office. I.P. Breazeal, who was the company bookkeeper, is shown holding Stanford, his son. Breazeal also ran the commissary in the company's lumber camp north of Farmerville in 1912. (Courtesy Janet Bowlin Phillips.)

Spearsville farmer and inventor Grady Hollis is pictured with one of his most popular inventions in the Spearsville community. His cultivator was easier to adjust for any specific task than any on the market. He will, however, forever be known worldwide as the inventor of a gadget called the Grabbit, which is in many households today. The device is an extension of the arm that allows users to retrieve objects from the ground without having to bend over to pick them up. Grady and his partner, Jimmy Lane Davis, sold the patent on the Grabbit for $50,000. Many companies make this tool today under a multitude of names. (Courtesy Calvin Hollis.)

In the early 1980s, oil spills made headlines. There were no efficient methods of retrieving the oil until Calvin Hollis and his partner Leon Taylor came up with a machine that solved the problem. In 1987, they sold their patent to the owners of Dollar General Stores. Calvin is the son of Grady Hollis. (Courtesy Calvin Hollis.)

Five

DOWNSVILLE AND SOUTHERN UNION PARISH

Mail carrier Wade Hampton Holman is shown on his rural route at the McDaniel place near Downsville in the early 1920s. The horse and buggy was the usual mode of delivering the mail to rural customers until the automobile eventually replaced it. (Courtesy Vivian H. Gray.)

During the 1920s, hats were an important part of the attire, as demonstrated by these folks from the Downsville area. Obviously, the hats were more for looks than for serving any practical purpose. The ladies are, from left to right, Dove Hale, Willa Ward, and Gina Ward accompanied by Bud Bryan and Dr. Fuller. (Courtesy Ann Hale Ballard.)

Ballard's Grocery, as it is known today, served the community of Downsville for many years throughout the 1950s and 1960s. During the 1930s, it was run by Fred Hamilton and Jim Hinton. In the later years, Jimmie and Ann Haile Ballard ran it. (Courtesy Louise Roberts Averitte.)

These philosophers in Downsville in the 1890s are, from left to right, Dr. James Meriweather Hamilton, Malcolm McFarland, Dr. R.H. Scaife, and ? Tidwell. Drs. Meriweather and Scaife were two of the four doctors in Downsville at the time. Tidwell ran the blacksmith shop in Downsville. (Courtesy Julia Holman McFarland.)

Located on the banks of D'Arbonne in Colson was the home of Dr. Henry Elliott Gates. Behind his home was a building where he made his own medicines. From the early 1880s, he served the communities around Colson until his death in 1913. Many Sunday mornings were spent patching up ruffians who had been injured in fights the night before. (Courtesy Freddie Gates.)

The courting pair of Edgar Johnson and Lillie Bayles is taking a buggy ride in this photograph from about 1914. On October 20, 1916, they were married, and son Lavelle was born on September 16, 1917. What life-changing events that buggy ride had for this pair. (Courtesy Louise Roberts Averitte.)

L.B. Carter, who owned and operated a store in Point, hauled freight and passengers on his boat from West Monroe to Point landing in the 1920s. Bayou D'Arbonne was the main mode of transporting goods in the late 1800s and early 1900s, whether by steamboats, flatboats, or private boats. Steamboats that traveled the Bayou needed at least 12 inches of water, while flatboats could navigate safely in less. (Courtesy of Diane Carter Mears.)

L.B. Carter is shown in about 1911 with his family and his wagon loaded with cotton to be carried to market. In front are, from left to right, L.B., sons Delma and Ollie, his wife, the former Willie Ann Powell, and his mother, Frances. On top of the wagon is Tinsley Jackson. (Courtesy Diane Carter Mears.)

Grover, Tom, Robert, and John Terry, along with George Terral and the Terrys' dog Sal are pictured at Francis Creek located on D'Arbonne in 1909. Their mode of travel is canoes fashioned from logs. This art of making dugout canoes was surely learned from Native Americans and passed down through generations. (Courtesy Roslyn Johnson.)

Susie B. Hale anxiously awaits a buggy ride in Downsville. Simple pleasures of life, such as buggy rides, were enjoyed during the early 1900s. It seems that folks today are missing some of the finer things in life enjoyed back then. (Courtesy Ann Hale Ballard.)

The logging crew of Levi H. Powell operated in the Point-Wilhite area of Union Parish in the early 1900s. (Courtesy Sandra Bales Littleton.)

During the 1920s, Hamp Holman owned and operated a portable sawmill in the Downsville area. Notable is the size of the saw blade used to cut the logs. Locals relied on this mill for lumber to build sheds, barns, and homes. (Courtesy Julia Holman McFarland.)

Henry Hiram Rugg owned and operated a sawmill on his farm near Rugg's Bluff. This scene at Rugg's mill is of Liddie Bullock Long Rugg at right and her husband, Henry Hiram Rugg, on the mule next to her. Lane Hicks, riding the mule in front of Rugg, worked at the mill. (Courtesy Roslyn Terry Johnson.)

Pictured at Rugg's mill in the back are Liddie Bullock Long Rugg and Henry Hiram Rugg. In front of them are Pearlie Long (Terry) and Velma Long (Averitte), her daughters from her first marriage to Dennis Long. (Courtesy Louise Roberts Averitte.)

During the 1940s, the cotton gin in Downsville was a busy place in the fall. Fred Hamilton owned and operated the gin there for many years until raising cotton became so unprofitable in the hill country that farmers turned to raising cattle and pine trees. (Courtesy Julia Holman McFarland.)

The Point baseball team of the late 1940s was called the Point Red Sox or the Point Night Owls, according to who you asked. Shown are (first row) Palmer Hinton, Hugh Orien Tidwell, Huey Antley, Chester Hinton, Harry Foster, Vic Antley, and Doyle Carter; (second row) Fulton Bayles Smith, Antley Ralson Nolan, Harry Maxey, Aubrey Antley (manager), Robert Kennedy, Ed Simpson, Christy Bayles, and unidentified (coach). (Courtesy Diane Carter Mears.)

The first telephone switchboard in Downsville was housed in the home of John Edwards. It was moved to the home of Alva and Beulah McMoy (pictured) in about 1924. The crank phones were installed in many homes in the area. Cranking the phone rang a bell to get the operator, who would ask, "What number please?" The caller then gave her the number of the person he wished to speak to, and the operator would connect the caller. (Courtesy Ann Hale Ballard.)

The donkey named Jim was the Averitte family school bus that transported the children down McDonald Road to Downsville High School in the 1920s. From left to right, neighbor Mary McDonald holds Jim while Lillian, Verma, and Victor sit astride. Their mother, Velma, is picking the cockle burrs from his tail so Jim will not buck the children off if he were to accidently swish a burr into his side. (Courtesy Louise Roberts Averitte.)

Another of the public school system's first schools was Rocky Branch. It served the area until 2006 when consolidation occurred and the students transferred to Farmerville. The building shown was replaced in time with a modern structure. The school offered the full 12 grades of education for many years. The building stands empty now, but the residents of Rocky Branch hope to get a school back in the near future. (Courtesy Union Parish Library.)

Holmesville School was located about six miles south of Farmerville on Highway 15. It was among the first public schools created when the public school system first began. Like the other first schools established in the parish, its exact location was to a large degree determined by the availability of water. (Courtesy of Union Parish Library.)

These students of Holmesville School in 1936 are (first row) Ella Mae, Marie Hicks, Florence Tatum, and Janelle Skains; (second row) Earline Cox, Mammie Tatum, Idabelle Skains, Geraldine Spurlock, Melva Bridges, Christine Gulledge, Heroice Cox, Opal Roy, and Hazel Cox. (Courtesy Linda Long Pardue.)

Mt. Ararat School was located three miles west of Point and was among those established to serve the area when the public school system was initiated. Mt. Ararat was among the many small schools throughout the parish that only offered grades through the seventh and had teachers leading multiple grades. (Courtesy Union Parish Library.)

The teaching staff of Downsville High School in 1923 is pictured from left to right: (first row, seated) Bebe Kilpatrick (in black), Sue Henry, Edith Miles, and Bess Henry; (second row) Mary Hinton, Leon Short, ? Buchman, Grace Jones, Fern Brantley, Lolita Golden, and Principal R.H. Hardage. (Courtesy Ann Hale Ballard.)

Typical of early-1900s construction was the Oliver and Stellar Johnson Pope home built near Wilhite. High ceilings and large windows allowed for cooling in the summer, while a large fireplace in the living room provided warmth in the winter. The steep roof prevented snow, or at least some of it, from blowing under the cypress shingles and into the attic. In most cases, there were no ceilings, so residents could wake up covered with snow if the wind was blowing. (Courtesy of Verline Hammons.)

The Downsville Post Office serves a large portion of the southwest part of Union Parish because of its isolated location. This is a photograph of the building as it looked in the 1950s. The post office first opened in Downsville on June 9, 1851, and was located in Philemon Wilhite's store, which was the common practice in those days. Wilhite served as postmaster until 1865. (Courtesy Julia Holman McFarland.)

In 1946, James Edward "Red" Hamilton built and ran this café in Downsville. This was a favorite meeting place for men to gather for coffee each morning and catch up on the latest news around town in the 1940s and 1950s. (Courtesy Julia Holman McFarland.)

The town of Downsville was incorporated in 1972. This panoramic view of Downsville shows the busy part of town in the 1970s. The post office and the corner store were the main attractions here. Downsville should remain viable for many years because of its remote location. (Courtesy Lallage Golden.)

The Masonic lodge was organized in Downsville on February 12, 1856. The first building was constructed of logs. The second was a two-story building that burned in 1921. The building shown here served until 1978 when the current brick building was constructed. (Courtesy Louise Roberts Averitte.)

The new Masonic lodge along with the Downsville Community Center is located in downtown Downsville. Lodge No. 143 is very active in Downsville, and many events are held at the community center year round. (Courtesy Louise Roberts Averitte.)

The Downsville Baptist Church building (at right) was constructed in 1916. In 1936, it was wired for electricity, and the educational wing was added in 1951. This building has served the community well for over 95 years. To the left stands the new modern First Baptist Church as it appears today. (Courtesy Ann Hale Ballard.)

New converts of Brother McMurry at a revival at Cross Roads Baptist Church are shown being baptized at Phillips Ferry on Bayou D'Loutre in about 1928. Pictured are, from left to right, Pete Nolan (son of Sandy Nolan), Willard Nolan, Dick Nolan, Joe Ollie Meeks, Docie Meeks, Mabel Nolan, Bo Nolan, Rella Kilcrease, Ola Dean, Velma Nolan, Elsie M. Gardner, Ella Patrick, Prud Gardner, Lois Nola, Cora Malone, Brother McMurry, Pete Nolan (son of Art Nolan), Aris Laster, Clyde Dean, Pete Meeks, Zollie Nolan, Earl Bailey, and Loyal Laster. (Courtesy of Jimmy Dean.)

The dedication service for the Holmesville Baptist Church was held on September 5, 1954. The building had been completed, and the note for money used to finish the church was burned at that service; the church was debt free. (Courtesy Linda Long Pardue.)

The First Methodist Church was established in Downsville in September 1866. Some years later, the building burned. The present site was secured, and Reverend Collier, an accomplished carpenter, led in the construction of a new church in 1890. Most of the furnishings, such as the pulpit and altar, were made by Reverend Collier. In 1953 and 1954, the present sanctuary and educational facilities were completed. (Courtesy Lallage Golden.)

A Baptist Church that serves the black community is located on the south side of Downsville. Rev. D. Lane Hicks, a white Baptist minister, is credited with helping organize the church. The church's Lane's Chapel is named in his honor. It started as a brush arbor, but the structure today is a large, brick building. Rev. C. Moss served the church for 26 years. In 1893, Rev. J.D. Davis was called to pastor. Today, the membership has grown to 165. (Courtesy Lallage Golden.)

This baptizing took place in Bayou D'Arbonne at Lake Drain in about 1919. Brother J.B. Mewborn is baptizing Stein Antley, unidentified, Ella Guice, unidentified, Tina Antley, and Eunice Allen. (Courtesy of Diane Carter Mears.)

The First Church came to Rugg's Bluff by 1917. Those pictured are, in no particular order, David Rugg, Barnie Pardue, Errin Rugg, Charlie Rugg, Myrtle Powell, Ester Pardue, Cecil Powell, Elsie Williamson, Alice Powell, Lou Dumas, Ella Dumas (with baby Clyde Dumas), Jo Dumas Bayles, Sallie Williamson, Ev Powell, Bessie Pardue, Annie Pardue, Ethyle Powell, Maybell Pardue, Mary Marley, Gertie Williamson, Becky Pardue, Ernie Powell, Jim Smith, Vince Bayles, Lizzie Rugg, Buck Dumas, Ben Pardue, Wiley Tidwell, Bud Rugg, Doc Pardue, Will Williamson, Dalton Williamson, and Jim Williamson. (Courtesy Louise Roberts Averitte.)

The Howard family band is seen here in about 1960. The "Hardy" Howard family loved their music. All of Hardy's sons learned to play an instrument. Those pictured are, from left to right, Brodus Smith on guitar, Kelton on bass, Hardy on fiddle, Verna on organ, Alton on guitar, and Jack on banjo. (Courtesy Roslyn Johnson.)

Civil War veterans from throughout Union Parish traveled to Mississippi to attend a reunion in 1921. They include (first row) Williamson Cobb, J.T. Spurlock, Billy Brantley, ? Parker, and unidentified; (second row) Bob Reynolds, Billy Crow, Jim Anderson, J.W. Terry, Phil Bearden, Bill Cole, ? Swafford, Ben Wallace, and two unidentified. (Courtesy Julia Holman McFarland.)

Visit us at
arcadiapublishing.com

· ·

www.ingramcontent.com/pod-product-compliance
Lightning Source LLC
Chambersburg PA
CBHW050605110426
42813CB00008B/2463